WHY MEN SHOULDn't HAVE SEX BEFORE MARRIAGE

CELLUS HAMILTON

ISBN: 9798344917177 (Paperback)
Imprint : Independently published

While this book is based on real events, experiences, and people, all names and identifying details have been changed to protect the privacy and confidentiality of individuals involved.

Book design by Mr.TK
Formatting design by Mulyana D-Zign

Published by Sow and Tell in the United States of America.

First printing edition 2024.

42 Tiemann Pl
Suite 418 New York,
NY 10027
www.cellushamilton.com

CellusHamilton.com

Listen to Cellus Hamilton's charting album
"Washing Her Feet"
for relevant music about love, sex,
covenant, & purity

DEDICATION:

To my sons Simeon & Marcellus, godsons Dawson
Amari Blake Smith & Eli James Stephens, and all of the men
around the world who will submit their whole selves
to the LORD—including their bodies.

————

TABLE OF CONTENTS

Introduction:
Why This Question Matters For Every Man 9

Chapter 1:
Immediate Repercussions: What Happens Right After 18

Chapter 2:
The Ripple Effect 41

Chapter 3:
The Dark Side of Premarital Sex 66

Chapter 4:
Laying the Groundwork: Marriage and Long-Term Happiness 93

Chapter 5:
A Life of Fulfillment: The Positive Effects of Abstinence 120

Chapter 6:
A Sacred Act: The Spiritual Dimension of Sex 166

Chapter 7:
The Challenge - Why and How to Practice Abstinence 171

Chapter 8:
The Bigger Picture: Why Your Choices Matter 194

Conclusion:
Taking the Next Step: Moving Forward with Purpose 219

INTRODUCTION

Why This Question Matters For Every Man

There are many reasons why men shouldn't have sex before marriage. And because it is not a one-sentence answer, the answer will be uncovered throughout this book. The reasons are so numerous that if you are currently sexually active, I believe you will be planning to make a life change after reading this book. Although my beliefs about sex being reserved for marriage between a man and a woman are central to this book, the principles of sexual discipline, respect for oneself and others, and the pursuit of a fulfilled life through abstinence are relevant to every man, regardless of their sexual orientation or personal beliefs. You don't have to be a Christian or follow a particular religion to understand the importance of sexual purity and how it can positively impact your life.

Though I talk a lot about marriage in this book and use it as a significant example of the damage caused by premarital sex, I want to make it abundantly clear that remaining pure and abstinent is not only for those who desire a healthy marriage. I want to point out that marriage isn't the goal for every man reading this book. Marriage is an extraordinary commitment and not something everyone should pursue. While marriage is deeply affected by premarital sex because it's so personal and relational, it's just one area where the impact is felt. In other words, men who don't desire marriage or never go on to get married will still have significant troubles and issues in their lives due to their decisions to engage in premarital sex. Premarital sex will affect all of their relationships, both friendly and familial. That is precisely how far and wide the effects of premarital sex go. That is why I feel the call to write this book. I feel this because sex is one of those areas where one decision has a compound effect on every other area of our life, whether we realize it or not. Though I was honest when I said earlier that you don't need to be a Christian or religious person to value and pursue a life of purity, I should be upfront and honest about the fact that I am an evangelist. While I would love for every man who picks up this book to read it in its entirety and apply the things written within its pages actively, I understand that there are other options. But if I'm completely honest, I secretly have an even deeper goal and desire for you.

My greatest and deepest desire would be that you would feel the calling and beckoning of a loving God who desires you to know Him and walk with Him every day of your life. This God is sovereign over the universe, created you, and knows everything about your life. He is the God who empowers you to do the very thing you are searching for within the pages of this book. I hope that every man reading this book will encounter Him. It would be a shame for us to settle for externally pure lives while remaining internally impure. And what a shame it would be for us to put into practice all the work and practical tips included within these pages while forfeiting eternal life with a loving God. Especially

 Why men shouldn't have sex before marriage

One who gave us an invitation in every page and chapter of this book. While you may be reading this book without any desire for a God encounter, I need you to understand that true purity cannot be obtained without first saying "yes" to a pure God. And as far as pure gods go, there is only one. And my prayer is that you say yes to Him.

But in a world that often idolizes marriage and places marriage on a pedestal as man's chief marker and indicator of success, it is very necessary for me to debunk this ideology and distance it from my own. In many ways, you will hear me describe how the call to remain pure should not be due to the avoidance of consequences or even in an attempt to gain certain rewards but that it should be done out of devotion to the God who created us and desires for us to live pure lives in the first place. One of the final statements that I'll make about this is that a selection of the men who have offered their reflections and stories are intentionally not married to show how the call to live pure is not only possible but also beneficial for those men who may read this book and never enter into a marriage relationship. Our pursuit of purity should not be because one day we hope to be pure for marriage but ultimately because we desire to be pure for God. Whether you are reading this book simply because the title intrigued you or whether you are a person lacking sexual discipline and desperately seeking help to make a change, this book has something for you.

This conversation is for everyone, regardless of where you stand. It even has much to say to the person who has not had sex before. To the young man who is actively in a place where he is still charting the path and the future in which he will direct his life, this book has much to say to you that will be helpful as you make that decision in the area relating to sex. And for those of us who may have only understood sexual purity as being deeply connected to religion, I want to encourage you that the life of abstaining from sex is not only something that religious people or Christians practice but that it is beneficial for people of all faith practices and backgrounds. In fact, in America, we are uniquely living in a time where more people are abstaining from sex not for spiritual reasons but because of how harmful it is to their lives. Beyond personal consequences, our collective sexual choices influence the moral fabric of our society. By embracing abstinence, we contribute to creating a culture that values respect, responsibility, and the well-being of all its members. At any rate, this book supersedes the boundaries of culture, ethnicity, sexual orientation, faith, and age. It boils us down to one simple category: men. And I believe every man was created for a purpose. To faithfully fulfill our purpose, we must face the reality that one of the greatest deterrents to us accomplishing what we are put on this earth to do is our lack of sexual discipline.

Sex may be perhaps the biggest distraction for men and one of the greatest and most common reasons why they often fail to reach their true potential. Sex is one of the most powerful forces in our world. It's a word that instantly grabs attention, no matter where it appears. Our fascination with sex isn't just about physical attraction; it's about how it influences culture, relationships, and even the direction of society. By understanding this power, we can better navigate its impact on our lives. For those of you who may be convinced that sex is merely physical, this book will reveal to you that sex is spiritual as well. Actually, it is more spiritual than physical. As we uncover the layers and the research of this truth, we encourage you to understand that there is more to our sexual lifestyles than meets the eye.

This journey will require self-reflection and a commitment to personal growth. I challenge you, the reader, to hold yourself accountable as you explore the contents of this book, knowing that the choices you make today will shape your future. I also want to be mindful that there may be a man who is reading this book who finds himself tempted to be discouraged and who feels like there is no hope for his future due to the sexual decisions he has made in his past. Not only do I believe that this book has much to say to you, but I also would love to encourage you that as long as you still have breath in your body, you have an opportunity to make new, wise decisions that God will reward in the future. A significant point that I would like to make, though, is that I encourage you as the reader not to decide to be sexually abstinent solely based on a fear of the consequences but out of a deep spiritual longing for God.

One of the fine lines I must navigate in writing this book is the line between legalism and being led by the Spirit of God. A person who does the right thing only because they do not want the consequences will not remove or avoid them. This is because the LORD desires us to do the right thing, not just to prevent the consequences but out of our love for Him. Inevitably, there will be two groups of people at the conclusion of this book. The first group will be men who believe they can take the information I have provided in this book, divorce it from any of its spiritual implications and connections, and faithfully pursue a life of purity and abstinence solely due to their human discipline and willpower. The men in this group will become painfully aware of their inability to live pure lives. They will be men who have discovered that even their best attempts to pursue purity and abstinence fall short without a spiritual heart change.

The second group of men will be those who discover that a personal and intimate relationship with Jesus is the secret to living a pure life. I hope that you will become a member of this second group. While this book serves a purpose to tackle the topic of purity, I am not naive in understanding that this book and everything it is asking and commissioning you to do is impossible without a deep relationship and transformation from the Lord Jesus Christ. I also would like to challenge the reader of this book to commit to remaining abstinent, at least until you finish reading this book. For those who may be reading this and are sexually active, this book will only be as beneficial as you prioritize it and give it room to be tested and applied to your life. I believe this challenge places both the author and the reader on a level playing field where my words may be carefully considered in a way that may transform your life forever. I believe this challenge is also fair to the reader because it allows them to know that if, at the end of this book, they are not yet convinced that sex should only be reserved for the marital relationship, then at the end of this book, they are free to live their lives as they have chosen. I truly believe that we are held accountable for the information we know. With that being said, if you would like to continue having sex without knowing about the damaging harm that you are bringing to yourself every time you engage in sex, then I encourage you to stop reading this book. Again, we are held accountable for everything that we learn. I believe in a God who is merciful. Every man who continues to live a sexually active lifestyle outside of marriage after reading this book is on their own. There is nothing more that I can do for you. At that point, you are choosing to live with the consequences of your actions, and we can both agree to respect that.

In today's world, perspectives on sex vary widely. On one hand, some believe that exploring multiple partners is the key to understanding what they want in a relationship. On the other hand, there's the belief that waiting until marriage provides the deepest, most fulfilling connection. This book will dive into these contrasting views, helping you understand each approach's long-term impact. In organizing this book, I decided to list the

  Why men shouldn't have sex before marriage ————————

reasons in the order of how soon you might feel the results. This organization will help sexually active readers realize how they are currently hurting themselves right now while also deterring those who are not sexually active. In addition to serving a purpose for the reader, this organization will show the many different effects and how they will impact our lives over time. Premarital sex carries consequences that go far beyond the physical. There are emotional, psychological, and even spiritual repercussions that many people don't consider until it's too late. In this book, we'll explore these consequences in depth, showing how each decision we make regarding sex can have lasting effects on our well-being and future happiness.

Chapter 1 will discuss the physical and emotional impacts of sex before marriage, including research from leading professionals and even interviews and stories from men that we can all learn from. One of the most incredible things about this book is that it includes personal narratives from men who have been careful to reflect on their lives and the decisions they made before they were married and to offer those insights and reflections. I have carefully chosen to anonymously include their reflections and personal narratives to protect these very intimate details of their lives. Where names are necessary, I have carefully replaced real names with created ones. I believe in more than mere information transfer. Wisdom is found in the men who have gone before us. One of the greatest places we can learn, especially about topics as important as purity, is from other men. There is no reason to reinvent the wheel. For generations, men have lived lives that we can learn from if we intentionally and carefully do so. So, as you are reading this book, please pay close attention to the personal narratives and stories in its pages. More than just my words, this book has been a collaborative effort of men who have already been committed to praying for you and imparting wisdom that can transform your life as a reader.

Chapter 2 will then make clear how premarital sex affects our relationships and how it affects things like trust, intimacy, and long-term relationship stability. We will encounter interviews with men who have real-life examples of relationships that struggled due to their decisions to have premarital sex. And we will also uncover how these issues can lead to a cycle of unhealthy relationships. Continuing from there, chapter 3 will examine the link between premarital sex and sexual violence, revealing shocking connections between premarital sex and higher incidences of sexual violence and abuse. As with every other chapter, we will also encounter research that links early sexual activity with increased vulnerability to abuse, and we will discuss how both victims and perpetrators are often caught in destructive cycles stemming from premarital sex.

Chapter 4 will look at the long-term impact on marriage and marital happiness as we analyze how premarital sex affects marriage quality, trust in a marriage, and even marital satisfaction. Again, we will encounter research on divorce rates and marital happiness, and we will compare and contrast stories from those who abstained versus those who didn't. We will even read some real accounts of men who faced challenges in their marriages due to past sexual experiences. Continuing to chapter 5, we will talk about "the better life" and how abstinence leads to fulfillment. We will make the case that abstaining from sex until marriage leads to better overall life satisfaction. This will be backed up with research, and we will also hear stories from men who have chosen abstinence and how it has positively impacted their lives. As I've emphasized before, there is a spiritual component to sex, which we explore in chapter 6. To explore this spiritual connection, we will use Genesis chapter 3 as a foundation and a blueprint to facilitate a deeper understanding of why sex is spiritual. We will also examine the spiritual implications of this and be met with examples of how understanding this connection can lead to healthier decisions.

In Chapter 7, we will move from the intellectual into the practical as we discuss why and how to practice abstinence. Lastly, we will bring all of these components together to show how they all work together and what they ultimately mean for our future, the decisions we make, and where this brings us when considering the object of our faith. I didn't come to these conclusions lightly. Through my own experiences, the stories of countless men I've encountered, and a deep study of the consequences of our sexual choices, I've come to understand just how pivotal this issue is in shaping the lives of men everywhere. Let's be honest: abstaining from sex isn't easy. The physical and emotional desires are real, and they can be overwhelming. However, acknowledging these challenges is the first step in overcoming them. This book doesn't shy away from the struggles you may face, but rather, it offers practical advice and encouragement to help you along the way. It's never too late to make a change. No matter what your past looks like, there's always hope for a better future. This book isn't about judgment; it's about helping you find a path that leads to true fulfillment and peace. The rewards can be life-changing if you're willing to take the journey.

CHAPTER 1:

Immediate Repercussions:
What Happens Right After

Embarking on a journey toward understanding why men shouldn't engage in premarital sex involves delving into both immediate and long-term impacts. From the outset, it's crucial to acknowledge that the reasons for abstaining extend beyond mere avoidance of negative consequences. Rather, they stem from a deeper commitment to personal and spiritual growth.

This book addresses the multifaceted nature of sexual discipline and purity, emphasizing that these principles are relevant to all men, regardless of their faith or personal beliefs. While Christian values inform my perspective, the core message—respecting oneself and others—transcends religious boundaries. Whether or not you identify with a particular faith, understanding the broader implications of sexual behavior is vital.

In the exploration of this topic, it's important to recognize that the decision to abstain from sex is not a means to a transactional end. We are not pursuing purity to receive something from God, but rather because of a genuine love for Him and a desire to lead a life of integrity and fulfillment. This commitment, however, does not ignore the practical realities and immediate consequences that arise from sexual choices.

As we begin this discussion, we'll address how premarital sex impacts men in the short term. The emotional and physical repercussions are real and can be profound, affecting not only one's well-being but also influencing relationships and self-perception. This chapter will uncover how these effects manifest and why understanding them is crucial for making informed decisions about one's sexual conduct.

For those who may have overlooked the introduction or are diving straight into the heart of the issue, this chapter serves as a critical starting point. It presents a candid look at the immediate consequences of premarital sex, setting the stage for a deeper exploration of how these experiences shape our lives and relationships.

By acknowledging these challenges upfront, we pave the way for a more comprehensive discussion on how to navigate the complexities of sexual discipline. This approach ensures that the practical aspects of abstinence are understood in the context of their broader, more impactful implications. Let's delve into these immediate consequences and explore how they underscore the importance of making thoughtful and intentional choices about sex.

The back of almost every pack of condoms has a sentence that says something like this: "This product does not protect against HIV/AIDS, other STIs, or pregnancy 100%." This sentence speaks volumes about how many of us try to live our lives. We put heavy faith into things that cannot guarantee 100% protection.

And this is at the heart of our physical and health challenges when it comes to sex. While condoms can significantly reduce the risk of STIs, HIV/AIDS, and unintended pregnancies, they are not 100% effective. Many people still contract infections or face unplanned pregnancies despite using protection. The only way to make sure to avoid sexually transmitted infections, HIV/AIDS, and unplanned pregnancy is abstinence. Abstinence is the very counter to the sentence on the packet of condoms. It provides 100% protection.

Even though we live in a time of significant advances in medicine and healthcare, the pain of suffering from an STI is still something anyone should want to avoid. According to the CDC, nearly 68 million people in the US have an STI, with 26 million new infections each year. Simply because bacterial infections like chlamydia, gonorrhea, and syphilis can be cured with antibiotics, many people take their sexual health less seriously. Studies show more people are contracting these infections even though treatments have improved. In 2022 alone, new syphilis cases among adults aged 15-49 increased by over 1 million, and there were 230,000 syphilis-related deaths worldwide.

If we applied this same logic to any other context, it would be easier to see how flawed it is. I don't know many people who would recklessly drive because they know hospitals can treat car accident injuries. While medical treatment is available for injuries, this mindset ignores the potential for severe consequences, including long-term damage or death, which can't always be mitigated by medical care. People are intentional about avoiding those risks yet do not take the same level of care when it comes to their sexual health. And to be clear, certain bacterial STIs are, in fact, painful. Gonorrhea and chlamydia can cause painful urination and testicular pain. Syphilis, in its later stages, can cause painful sores, rashes, and muscle aches. Chancroid causes painful ulcers on the genitalia.

Another important fact is that once infected by an STI, it becomes easier to contract another one. Studies show that changes in the genital tract caused by STIs like gonorrhea and chlamydia can make it easier for new infections to take hold. Co-infections are another concern; having one STI can increase the likelihood of acquiring another. For example, ulcerative STIs like syphilis or herpes can provide an entry point for other infections, including HIV. Overall, some STIs weaken the immune system or cause chronic inflammation, making it harder for the body to fight new infections. Geoffrey P. Garnett, Ph.D., and Francis J. Bowden conducted research on behalf of the American Sexually Transmitted Diseases Association, showing that men can often have infections like chlamydia without any symptoms. This makes it easier for the infections to go unnoticed and spread. Their findings suggest that avoiding risky behaviors, such as premarital sex, can be an effective way to reduce the chances of contracting these hidden infections that are not always caught through regular health screenings. This should be enough to make anyone concerned. According to the World Health Organization, HIV, viral hepatitis epidemics, and sexually transmitted infections cause 2.5 million deaths each year and continue to pose significant public health challenges.

Research from experts like Marcus Y. Chen and Sepehr N. Tabrizi further highlight how sexually transmitted infections (STIs), particularly in men, are becoming harder to treat as bacteria like *Neisseria gonorrhoeae* and *Mycoplasma genitalium* develop resistance to antibiotics. These infections can cause painful symptoms and increase the risk of more serious diseases like HIV. As resistance spreads, effective treatment becomes more challenging, emphasizing the importance of preventing infection in the first place.

A study in a sexually transmitted disease clinic in Birmingham, AL, found that over a quarter of men aware of sexually transmitted infection symptoms delay seeking health care for over seven days. While we don't have the details of their reasonings for the delay, we do know that not all of them avoided sex after experiencing symptoms. For many, this level of irresponsibility operates on autopilot mode in a culture that is mindlessly controlled by its urges and societal pressures.

Even worse, this same reckless mindset extends to incurable viral STIs like HIV, herpes, and HPV. In 2024, California, Texas, New York, Florida, and Georgia had the highest reported STIs. Yet, some people still risk catching these viral diseases simply because medications can manage them. While medical advancements are a blessing, this has become less of a deterrent and more of an excuse for risky behavior. Managing illnesses is not the same as curing them. Additionally, the World Health Organization reports that the four curable STIs—syphilis, gonorrhea, chlamydia, and trichomoniasis—account for over 1 million infections daily. New data also shows that the variances in strains of gonorrhea have consistently grown resistant to its most common treatments, adding another layer of concern.

On top of this, certain groups face higher risks. Five key populations: men who have sex with men, people who inject drugs, sex workers, transgender individuals, and those in prisons or closed settings experience significantly higher HIV prevalence rates than the general population. Additionally, a poll conducted by Ohio State University in June 2024 revealed that one-third of Americans mistakenly believe STIs can only be transmitted through sexual intercourse, and 20% think testing is only necessary if they experience symptoms. This ignorance may be fueling the spread of infections.

Additionally, access to contraceptives and emergency contraception has made it easier for many to avoid the risk of bringing children into the world unprepared. Rather than fully considering the consequences of premarital sex, we often rely on the availability of birth control to justify our actions. We fail to consider the effects pregnancy has on a woman's body, and we overlook the value of the life that is being created or destroyed.

Unplanned pregnancies can significantly change a person's life and goals. Many men have to leave school, switch careers, or give up jobs they love. They might also have to put off traveling to focus on the unexpected responsibility of raising a child and managing their finances. Not only are these men forced to make drastic changes that often lower their quality of life and shift them directly into parenthood, but many also make these quick transitions out of their hobbies or passions during the prime times in their lives and careers. These pivots often leave them severely delayed in accomplishing their life goals or, even worse, completely prevent them from achieving them. Men who are impacted by unplanned pregnancies and forced into fatherhood often find themselves postponed in their careers at best, while others witness their personal goals, further education, or hobbies become altogether abandoned. This shift in their focus and reprioritization of resources can have long-term effects on their ambitions and subsequent lifestyle choices. Many of us are already aware of the statistics showing that men without a college degree or higher education are much more likely to live in poverty and be excluded from opportunities that require advanced learning credentials. Since an essential part of fatherhood is leaving a lasting legacy—emotionally, spiritually, and financially—a large population of men who enter fatherhood through unplanned pregnancy are often less capable of providing a quality legacy. This usually limits their children's prospects, reducing fatherhood to a menial level that doesn't position future generations to improve.

As of recent data, about one-third (32%) of children in the United States live with an unmarried parent, a significant increase from 13% in 1968. This trend is mainly due to declines in marriage rates and increases in births outside of marriage. Most children in these households live with a solo mother (21%), while others live with cohabiting parents (7%) or a solo father (4%).

To ignore the consequences of premarital sex, we have opted to sacrifice whatever is necessary to protect our personal and sexual freedom. Not only are we not good stewards of our own or women's bodies, but we also fail to care for our emotional health. While it is often not discussed, many men who have fathered an aborted child wrestle with the memory, no matter how much they try to forget it.

But what is most frightening about premarital sex is that we can never fully know what the consequences may be. And regarding STIs, we can't detect who is infected solely by the human eye. In many cases, men have not known they were having sex with someone who was infected until it was too late. By the time they had found out, they were already infected themselves and no longer able to go back in time and make a different decision. People with STIs do not have bright red labels on their foreheads saying, "Beware! I am an infected person". And due to shame, embarrassment, and the deep desire to be loved, few people are honest about their sexual health and history. For example, how many dates should you go on before you interrupt the evening by saying, "I really like you a lot, and I think we've got to know each other enough to share with you that I have red, itchy sores on my penis."? And while it is never ok to disrespect, reject, or judge someone based on their medical condition, why would we want to put ourselves in this position if we don't have to? I know several people with diseases and infections who wish someone would've told them the truth. They regret the money they've had to spend on medication and doctor's visits because they didn't have the information included in this book.

Every time a person engages in premarital sex, they are gambling with consequences. Another immediate consequence of premarital sex is the emotional and psychological effects. These emotional responses vary greatly depending on the individual's beliefs, values, cultural background, and personal experiences. Feelings of guilt and shame, anxiety, and regret can often arise after an individual has engaged in premarital sex. These emotions are usually connected to the individual having a strong desire or conviction against premarital sex that then comes in the wake of the realization of their actions. The feeling that a person may have gone against their values may result in an overwhelming feeling of guilt based on the belief that they have violated their religious or cultural beliefs. Then there can be a strong sense of shame and feelings that they are worthless, inadequate, or even stems from internalized beliefs or perceived judgment from others.

There is also the reality that many people, especially in the wake of premarital sex, experience fears and anxiety related to pregnancy, sexually transmitted infections, or the impact on the relationship. Men who are plagued with the uncertainty that they may have gotten someone pregnant or that they may have contracted a disease can often find themselves in such intense emotional anxiety that it affects their work, productivity, relationships, and even their ability to rest and get sleep. There is also the reality that many men immediately regret their decision. This regret can stem from the realities of men feeling that the sexual encounter was rushed, pressured, not meaningful, or not in line with their personal or moral values.

In my case, when I was sixteen years old and had finished having sex with my girlfriend, as the days passed, anxiety and regret very similar to what I have just described began to take over my mind. I was very regretful that I had tainted my Christian witness and that I had ruined the chance of proving to my girlfriend that there were men who were sincere about their values, convictions, and purity. I also felt deep guilt and shame that I had violated my covenant with God. And the ignorant man that I was at the time anxiously awaited punishment—believing that God was going to punish me for what I had done. I also felt an uneasy range of emotions as I waited for my girlfriend's next period, even though we had used a condom. And with every conversation about sex or sexually transmitted infections that I would encounter, I always had a lingering question in my mind. Still, I felt like I was too guilty and ashamed to take a test at the time. All of these emotions flooded me as a sixteen-year-old man, and they are all too familiar to sexually active men.

Many people who interact with porn, especially those not sexually active, often believe what they see is real. However, porn is a billion-dollar entertainment industry designed to sell sex, using Hollywood-style illusions to make it seem like an intense, perfect experience every time. My friend, whom God radically saved from the porn industry, shared his testimony with me. He was once entangled in a dark world of fast money, sex, and drugs, running an adult film company as one of his many side hustles. He revealed how many women in the industry are broken, depressed, and trapped by their circumstances. Often, they endure shame, exploitation, and multiple partners out of a desperate need for money or as a result of broken families. For some, the shallow flattery from strangers feels more like love than anything they have known. Most of these women are high on drugs to numb their pain, and many come from foreign countries, living as sex slaves in exchange for basic needs like food and shelter.

My friend explained that many porn scenes are edited to create the illusion of long, passionate encounters, while in reality, they are short and mechanical. It's important to highlight these falsehoods because they contribute to the unrealistic expectations around sex. People often say yes to sex, expecting it to match the intensity they see in porn, only to feel depressed and let down afterward. They search for the fulfillment promised by pornography, not realizing that what they seek can only be found elsewhere.

Even in committed, healthy sexual relationships like marriage, sex doesn't always match the fantasy. Married couples will tell you that moods vary and that intimacy is not always a thrilling escapade. The security of marriage removes the pressure for every encounter to be perfect, knowing that it won't be the last. The industry preys on this misunderstanding, which is why it continues to attract billions every year. As men, we must imagine the pain of knowing that the women being exploited could be our mothers, sisters, or wives. Every person is on a quest to be deeply known and loved, yet true fulfillment cannot be found in the illusions sold by pornography.

Sex often creates a strong emotional bond, which can lead to feelings of attachment. If these feelings aren't reciprocated, they can cause intense emotional pain. Because sex was designed to bond two people together, when it's used outside the covenant of marriage, it still tries to fulfill that purpose. However, this bonding in the wrong context can become harmful, leaving both individuals vulnerable. They may be more easily manipulated or emotionally hurt by each other or by others. Additionally, the intimacy of sex can lead to feelings of disposability, especially if the relationship lacks commitment or stability, which we'll explore further in the next chapter.

There is an old school phrase that says, "Why would a man work to get his license if he gets to drive the car without one?". Men often place women in vulnerable positions whenever we initiate or participate in sex outside of the covenant of marriage.

One of my good friends had a great head on his shoulder and was committed to the LORD and a lifestyle of purity. On that journey, he met a young lady he was attracted to, and they had a lot of great moments together, sharing common interests and excellent emotional compatibility and chemistry. However, this journey of getting to know one another was cut short once they began having sex. This intense physical interaction between them halted their exploration of one another and their learning of the value systems, beliefs, and stories that were part of them as individuals. It even threw them into a hazy confusion prompting them to ignore red flags, personality traits, and even apparent turnoffs that they would have otherwise responded and paid attention to had sex not been introduced.

As the relationship progressed, this man began to overlook things he had once promised himself he would never tolerate, all because of the pleasure and thrill of sex. Over time, their relationship shifted from communication, emotional compatibility, and shared interests to being centered around sex. This led them to falsely believe they were soulmates. It wasn't until after marriage, when the real work of understanding, loving, and committing to someone beyond physical intimacy began that he realized he had made a serious mistake. This is the kind of confusion that often arises when sex is introduced outside the covenant of marriage. Many couples become blinded by the pleasure of sex, unable to see each other clearly. It creates internal conflict, where actions contradict personal values, leaving individuals caught in the familiar struggle of "my mind is telling me no, but my body is telling me yes."

In my journey of mentoring young men, I've seen many stories where men are convinced that they should not be with a woman who is unhealthy for them, yet due to sex complicating the relationship, they find that there is an internal battle between actually doing the healthy thing for both parties and ending the relationship.

There's a whole population of people whose response to premarital sex leads to a sort of emotional detachment. For them, sex sparks the reality that not only do they not love or feel safe or connected with the person but that they sincerely don't want anything to do with the person at all and can even spill into all other relationships that have any sexual aspect or connotation to them. An example of this would be a man who experiences sex. As a result of his not feeling emotionally safe or connected with the partner of his sexual experience, he intentionally detaches himself from that individual and all other individuals who may be seeking to love him genuinely. This can lead to intense isolation and depression. The other side of this coin is that premarital sex, void of any covenant, can become easily understood as being the normative way that sex is and should be experienced. When this happens, it has the negative effect of making men numb. This is often seen in men who live their lives in promiscuity, running from sexual partner to sexual partner, always seeking an emotional connection but never finding one, while deeply believing that sex is designed to be something very casual and without any serious commitment involved. In many regards, this is where much of our culture and society falls due to the prevalence of premarital sex in a sexually active culture in our society. Many men have become numb to the point where they are no longer capable of experiencing emotional intimacy as it pertains to sex, partly because they have built a practice of approaching it casually and even being indoctrinated that sex does not need to be reserved for a committed relationship. In many respects, they are also being taught that sex should not have an emotional connection and that it is strictly physical, which could not be further from the truth. Many of us would assume this type of desensitization and numbness happens over a gradual period of time, and even though it does, this does not mean that only one time cannot lead to a level of numbness.

Amongst many people, there is an understanding and a connection made that once a person has engaged in sex, their value decreases. While this is usually rooted in hyper-religious cultures that shame and view sex as dirty and evil, it is true that premarital sex does have a negative impact on self-esteem for many people. There is also the fear of relationship changes. For someone who feels like they have the pressure of delivering an incredible sexual experience to keep their significant other, this pressure not only works against them but can also be the cause of why some people feel their relationship becomes less stable after sex is introduced. For couples that were once rooted in the mental, emotional, and spiritual commonalities between them, premarital sex can often cloud judgment.

Many of these above emotional conditions and changes are a result of having sex outside of a marriage covenant. They are proof that relationships experience much confusion whenever premarital sex is introduced. The sad part is that many people are unaware that they are hurting themselves and the person they claim to love.

Men who already have a more difficult time naming and understanding their emotions find themselves more emotionally unclear than they already were. These men shift drastically between several emotions at random times, which will often be expressed in unpredictable ways. Examples of these will be shifting quickly from excitement to anxiety or joy to depression. Many of these men will find themselves in a rat race of trying to solve the puzzle of their emotions by bandaging them with either more premarital sex or some other unhealthy habit that the culture has popularized. Because they are unaware that the source and fueling of their emotional confusion comes from premarital sex, they often feed into the lies that culture tells them, which is that premarital sex will ultimately solve their problems, make them feel better, and level out their emotions. And none of these are true.

While there is a cultural stigma that it is only women who are capable of feeling used or exploited regarding sex, men are not immune to these genuine feelings. Nowadays, with pop culture popularizing the "lady pimp" and encouraging women to "Act Like a Lady, Think Like a Man"—the cycle of emotional abuse in relationships has increased. The idea that women should understand and adopt certain traditionally masculine mindsets or strategies, especially in relationships, to navigate the dating world successfully is unnatural and unhealthy. Men in fact should be held responsible for their actions and should model the vulnerability and transparency they desire to see. And the idea that women will do better protecting themselves by conforming to the abusive men of a perverted culture is far from helpful.

For sexual encounters that are not mutual or consensual, it is easy for men to feel used or exploited, which harms men's confidence and deters them from pursuing relationships. Men feeling used or exploited can often lead to feelings of anger, betrayal, and deep emotional pain. While we often think of these responses as being something that can only stem from sexual violence or abuse, many consensual sexual relationships in which one person did not feel fully respected or considered can lead to them feeling used or exploited. I've even heard of situations where Christian men have expressed feeling taken advantage of by women who attempted to lessen their level of cognition through the use of alcohol or other recreational drugs.

Premarital sex also introduces a unique change in relationship dynamics as power may shift due to one person feeling more invested or in control. While generally, this is reserved for men in the areas of heterosexual relationships, women who feel like now they can control men by manipulating them with sex or using their bodies to blackmail men into submission is a prevalent thing. This dynamic is often not spoken of but has led many men astray into lifestyles, decisions, and perpetual habits that they would have never entered otherwise. It is also one of the reasons why men who have been engaged in premarital sex find themselves involved in tasks that were connected to previous relationships that they are no longer in, yet unable to detach from the tasks themselves.

For example, a man may find himself unable to say no to a woman who he is no longer in a relationship with simply because he has spent so much time relinquishing control over his own life due to the relationship dynamic that their sexual activity introduced. This is why non-physical abuse is often amplified once sex comes into the picture. Premarital sex and sexual activity, in general, have a unique way of bonding people in such a way that even after the relationship has dissipated, both people struggle to find the boundaries of where their individual life begins and another person's individual life ends. These blurred lines, imbalances, and relational rollercoasters come from premarital sex and are signs that it is not healthy for men to engage in this sort of activity outside of the marriage covenant. It is also a clear indicator that these are not the challenges that a loving, intentional, and divine God intended for His children. And we know this because of the Biblical command against this.

Though the consensus around premarital sex and sexual activity has rapidly changed in the Western hemisphere over the last several decades, there are still specific communities that value sexual purity and look down on premarital sex. Many of these communities exist in rural areas where there is strong tradition and a deep moral and religious ethos. In these locations, people who engage in premarital sex may be exiled from their families, churches, and jobs. They can experience isolation, rejection, shame, and being bullied. And because sin often is strengthened by the burden of heavy law, many people are forced to keep their sex lives a secret in order to prevent being ridiculed and ostracized. Sadly, many of those who most fervently enforce these strict premarital laws are often guilty perpetrators themselves. The people and citizens of these communities are spread far and wide, and many of them are women who automatically write off men who are not living a lifestyle of purity. Notably, many women who have themselves committed to a life of purity and abstinence naturally enforce the same discipline and devotion on the men that they consider for dating. These pressures mean that men who engage in premarital sex are instantly cutting themselves off from a population of women who are themselves disciplined, spiritually adept, and ripe for a healthy relationship.

One of the worst things hyper-religious communities have done has been to detach purity from its purpose and connection to God. They have shamed entire generations into doing the "right thing" for the "wrong reasons." And because our motivation for why we abstain is the most critical part of abstaining, we have flooded communities with people who are abstaining while hating their lives, their partners, and the communities that force this lifestyle on them. They abstain to avoid being disowned by their families, churches, and friends. And ultimately, the only way they believe they will ever be free is to either suffer in silence or to rebel. While many people live their lives in either one of these positions, the reality is that those who choose to rebel are often encouraged because they are embraced by a community that was shamed in the same way. This community loves them, accepts them, and offers them everything their families, churches, and friends failed to give them—unconditional love.

Many of us have heard stories about people who come from conservative and religious families who end up having an unplanned pregnancy. We've listened to the stories of parents rejecting their children, saying, "Because you didn't wait until you were married and do it my way, I'm no longer going to support you and your child. You must leave my home and figure it out on your own". These are genuine social pressures that come as an immediate and relatively quick result of premarital sex. However, the irony and messiness of these situations only reveal a broader issue. The statistics already show that premarital sex causes a plethora of problems for all involved, but those problems multiply whenever we shame people into abstaining rather than allowing them to decide on their own.

In the age of social media, this shame and how others view a person can quickly leave the traditional community boundaries and be extended to the internet's global reach. Harmful memes, posts, and threads calling out men and women for their promiscuity and slandering their reputations all over the world are also common, and risks must be considered. Thirty years ago, having premarital sex might've ruined your reputation in your school and city. Today, premarital sex can taint a man's reputation in his state, region, and nation. And sadly enough, as premarital sex has become more widely acceptable and honorable across cultures, the pursuit and value of having an honorable name has also dwindled. Today, there is a growing culture of men who wear sexual promiscuity and the number of women they've had sex with as a badge of honor. They make it their goal and are incredibly open about their sexual lifestyles. This growing group will inevitably experience the difficult consequences laid out in this chapter.

There are also many women who view men who have been sexually active as automatically not being a good man to marry. They believe that a man who has had sex will be less likely to be satisfied and pleased by them, and they avoid relationships with this kind of man to preserve and protect their security. In addition to these beliefs, many women also believe that a man who has a history of being sexually active and intimate with several women will be less likely to remain faithful in the marriage. While this judgment does not apply to all men, the research I have conducted while writing this book does support this difficult reality. Men who engage in premarital sex or experience sex with multiple women before getting married have a much higher chance of cheating on their wives. It also may become difficult to build trust and safety within the marriage; especially with women who value sexual exclusivity and purity.

One unspoken and more challenging reality is that men are fighting an unfair double standard often perpetuated by the culture and broader society. On one hand, men face extreme rejection, persecution, or bullying for not being sexually active. Amongst their peers and other men around them, their sexuality or manhood may be questioned if they are not sexually active. This is because popular culture has connected "being a man" with being sexually active and the conquering of women and their bodies. It has also frequently defined manhood strictly based on male anatomy and genitalia without considering the qualities, character, and sacrificial nature that manhood truly entails.

One man interviewed for this book shared how early exposure to hip-hop culture influenced his views on sex. He said, "The culture had an influence on me early on—starting as early as second grade, when I was introduced to hip-hop with Cash Money's *I Need a Hot Girl*. I knew the lyrics by heart when I was just seven or eight years old. The lyrics went:

> 'I like 'em hot,
>
> The ones that don't tell me to stop,
>
> Eat ****, swallow the ***,
>
> And they know how to pop.'

"Songs like that shaped my outlook and made me desire certain things. I wanted a 'hot girl.' Culture, my community, the area I was in, and the influence that was around me pushed me towards pursuing sex before marriage."

Another man I interviewed expressed a similar struggle. He said, "My cultural background definitely influenced my decision to have sex before marriage. The friends I had—I would get picked on and bullied if I still had my virginity, and that got old. I got tired of feeling left out. I got tired of feeling like I was less of a man. Society and our culture as Black people made you feel like you were less of a man if you hadn't experienced this. And something is wrong with you as a result, so you go after it and desire it to the point where you are using women to conquer them, versus having a real connection and relationship with them. My culture absolutely taught me to compromise my soul to please my flesh."

These examples show that men face extreme rejection, persecution, and bullying both for abstaining as well as for not living pure lives. They are placed in an impossible no-win situation. Men are made fun of for not having sex and then shamed, ridiculed, and thrown away when they give in to culture's

  Why men shouldn't have sex before marriage

pressure. This weight on men is a significant reason why a clear line must be drawn between purity culture and the true heart of purity. Purity culture promotes the lifestyle of purity while neglecting the heart posture of purity. It makes empty promises to people, assuring them that their lives and futures will be better as a result of them abstaining from sex. It claims that God owes us and will reward us based on our work of purity. This belief is incredibly dangerous because it fails to communicate the truth that God does not owe us anything. Our purity does not mean that we will be blessed with a spouse, good relationships, or even an incredible sex life later on. On the contrary, the actual benefits of living a life of purity are less tangible and are more invisible. It is the fruit of experiencing more peace and less anxiety daily.

Yet, in a Western culture where materialism and blessings are only measured by physical possessions, many have opted out of abstaining simply to obtain invisible blessings. They would instead trade their peace and physical health for money, power, companionship, and pleasure. After all, who cares about how my decision to have sex now will affect my life 10 years from now? And this is precisely the lie we have been continuously fed since Satan first introduced it in the garden. "You won't die". But the truth is that they *would* die, except that it would not be an immediate death but a gradual decay that eventually leads to death. Satan knew that after Adam and Eve took a bite of the forbidden fruit and waited a few moments for its consequences to kick in, he could convince them to keep eating. And just like Adam and Eve, many of us will continue to do what is killing us simply because the ultimate death promised is not immediate.

The truth is that there is no freedom found in the practice of abstinence or in the acts of premarital sex. Freedom is not tied to the "what" we do, but ultimately to the "why" we do it.

Your desire to have sex might leave you like it did it Noah. Here's Noah's story:

Noah was 19 years old and a kid who was always known for having everything together. He had grown up in church, always got good grades, played on all the sports teams, and excelled in academics and athletics. He was not considered a nerd because of his athletic ability but also had friends in many diverse spheres. He got along well with the most popular kids in school and those who were ostracized and no one wanted anything to do with. Noah was the middle child out of three boys. And he had grown up with both parents in a very stable home. Noah's parents raised him and taught him the importance of saving himself for marriage. While he had grown up having innocent puppy love relationships with women, he had always made sure that he never allowed himself to have sex. In fact, if it wasn't for Noah being so popular on his basketball team and with his grades, he probably would've been made fun of by his peers who didn't believe sex should be saved for marriage. However, because Noah was a leader, he lived without much influence from those around him. Eventually, Noah graduated from high school and enrolled in a midsize college in a small town in North Carolina.

This was Noah's first time away from home and was also his opportunity to grow and discover who he was as a man, away from the influence of his parents and familiar upbringing in Georgia. Like most people when they go to college, Noah was excited about the opportunity to experience this new level of independence and had always dreamed that college would be where he would meet his future wife. Unlike many people in college who surrounded Noah and were excited about the opportunity to have endless premarital sex, attend wild parties, and do all the things that their parents would never allow them to do back at home, Noah had determined in his mind that he

 Why men shouldn't have sex before marriage

was going to stay on the straight and narrow path during his time at college.

All of this continued until one day, Noah found himself spending a lot of time studying with a friend with whom he shared several classes. Their time together would often be innocent as they studied and poured over difficult study questions in their calculus and history classes.

Noah knew that this girl, who we'll call Mia, enjoyed going to parties and often would share with him stories about her sexual experiences with other men on campus—many of these men would even be Noah's friends.

Noah, being innocent and inexperienced, began to develop feelings for Mia and would even enjoy listening to these stories about her sexual experiences and would find himself being intrigued and, in a sense, high imagining the life that was all around him—that he had intentionally shielded himself from.

As time went on, Noah and Mia's study times became less and less about studying, as Noah secretly found himself hoping that one day something sexual would happen between them. Because Noah was shy and would never be the type of man to initiate this action on his own, several weeks went by during which Noah continued to meet up with Mia, hoping that one day she might see him as more than just a study friend.

One particular night, while Mia was sharing with Noah about her frustration with men who only want her for sex, Noah comforted Mia, which resulted in her sharing with him about how she felt that he was her only male friend who had never tried anything with her. She felt that Noah was her only friend who really loved her for her and that, ironically, this made her feel safest and more willing to give him her body than to any of the other men that she had been dealing with. Upon hearing this confession, Noah, who had been nervously dreaming for this moment, grew excited about the opportunity that had just been presented to him. Yet, he remembered how uncomfortable he had felt hearing many of her stories about how many men she had been with on campus.

With the rise of hormones and emotions, Noah and Mia had sex, and Noah ended up losing his virginity to Mia at the age of nineteen. After the sex was over, Noah suffered weird emotional feelings toward Mia. He wasn't sure if they were a couple, but he knew he greatly cared for her. He had a flood of mixed emotions. On one hand, he was excited that he wasn't a virgin anymore, but on the other hand, he was concerned because they had had unprotected sex. Unfortunately, Noah contracted HIV from Mia. And his life was never the same. He had only had sex one time, and he and Mia never ended up being together. Today, Noah spends his life sharing with young men and women about his life, his illness, medication, and ultimately, his regrets about the decision he now has to live with after his first time having sex.

CHAPTER 2:

The Ripple Effect

Some of the best decisions I've made in my life include saying yes to Jesus, committing to my wife in marriage, and choosing to wait until marriage to have sex with each other. Even though neither of us was a virgin when we met, we made the choice to honor God and each other by remaining abstinent until we were married. These decisions shape every part of my day. Because Jesus is the Lord of my life, I seek His guidance in how I spend my time. My marriage is the next filter, ensuring that my actions honor my wife, such as avoiding one-on-one time with other women unless we both agree and trust those involved.

Waiting to have sex until after marriage impacted our relationship in a powerful way. It allowed us to build a strong friendship and intimacy that keeps us grounded. Because of this choice, our marriage and our relationships with others remain pure and undefiled. This wasn't easy, and we aren't perfect, but making this commitment is possible for anyone willing to honor God and each other in their relationship.

These decisions don't just stand alone; they create a ripple effect that influences every part of my life. Every aspect of my daily life is impacted by my choosing to honor Jesus and my marriage. My schedule is shaped around time with God and my wife, my spending is filtered through our shared values and goals, and even my commitments to others are measured against how they align with these priorities. Just like a stone hitting water, these choices create ripples that touch everything—shaping my relationships, guiding my interactions, and setting a standard for how I live.

The phenomenon that I am speaking about, in which one decision impacts every other decision is called the ripple effect. It is called the ripple effect because, just like when an object comes in contact with water, an energy transfer initiated at the point of contact creates ripples that will continue infinitely until they hit a force strong enough to stop the ripple. And for many of us, before we can strategize and be intentional about the ripples we would like to create, we first must build the strong force that will stop the ripples our habits have already set in motion. This is imperative if we plan to "stay afloat"—as I attempt to keep the metaphor going.

The ripple effect of our choices can shape every corner of our lives, especially when it comes to our relationships. Waiting to have sex until marriage wasn't just a single decision; it set off a series of positive changes in how we relate to each other, our goals, and the kind of future we want to build together. But what happens when the choice goes the other way? How does premarital sex influence not only the dynamics of a relationship but also our aspirations and the long-term consequences we face? Let's explore these impacts in depth.

 Why men shouldn't have sex before marriage

In *Hooked: New Science on How Casual Sex is Affecting Our Children*, authors Joe S. McIlhaney Jr. and Freda McKissic Bush delve into the science behind sexual intimacy and its effects on emotional attachment. The book outlines how sexual activity initiates complex chemical processes in the brain that are designed to bond individuals on a deep, emotional level.

The authors emphasize the roles of oxytocin and vasopressin in this process. Oxytocin, often called the "bonding hormone," is particularly significant for women, as their brains have more receptors for it. During sexual intimacy, oxytocin creates feelings of closeness and attachment to the partner. Vasopressin performs a similar role for men, fostering protective and bonding instincts. These hormones, released even during a single sexual encounter, create a sense of attachment that can last for a long time.

Additionally, the release of dopamine during sex provides a sense of pleasure and reward, which reinforces the desire to repeat the behavior. While this bonding mechanism is beneficial in marriage—helping couples maintain a strong, lasting emotional connection—it can have detrimental effects when experienced in casual or premarital relationships. According to the book, repeated sexual encounters with multiple partners can weaken the brain's ability to form lasting attachments. This is due to the neural pathways involved in bonding becoming "trained" to break attachment, making it more difficult to connect deeply in future relationships.

For males, this biological bonding process serves as an essential argument for abstinence before marriage. Engaging in multiple sexual relationships can create a pattern that erodes trust, aligns intimacy improperly, and sets up communication barriers. The psychological effects can include a reduced capacity for commitment and an increased likelihood of relational dissatisfaction.

The book also points out that the prefrontal cortex—the part of the brain responsible for rational decision-making—does not fully mature until the mid-twenties. This immaturity, coupled with dopamine's reward-seeking behavior, means that teenagers and young adults are particularly susceptible to the risks associated with casual sex, highlighting the need for guidance in these formative years.

Ultimately, *Hooked* presents compelling evidence that human beings are "designed" for lifelong, monogamous relationships and that casual sexual behavior can undermine the very mechanisms intended to nurture and protect these bonds. This scientific perspective reinforces the argument for abstinence, illustrating how premarital sex can impact relationship dynamics, personal goals, and long-term emotional health.

From here, we can delve into how this science explains the erosion of trust, the misalignment of intimacy, communication barriers, and psychological consequences that arise from premarital sexual relationships.

One of the things about relationships is the merging of two different people from two different backgrounds who bring two different kinds of baggage into the central meeting place of a relationship. One person may have grown up in a home that emphasized specific values and expectations in a relationship. At the same time, the other had a completely different value system and set of expectations. In a culture where many people enter into relationships strictly based on superficial indicators such as attraction or where a person lives, many ignore the vital work of discovering what exists within a person's mind. This is incredibly detrimental, mainly because physical appearance and location are least likely to cause conflict or disagreement within the relationship. What is common and likely to cause a rift in the relationship is that both have different expectations and belief

 Why men shouldn't have sex before marriage

systems about what a relationship should include and what is necessary to maintain happiness and contentment.

While experts like Gary Chapman have conducted extensive research and introduced us to powerful concepts such as the five love languages and the five ways of apology, many partners enter into these expectations having hardly had any conversation about what the person desires in the relationship or where they plan for their life to end up. Yet, unfortunately, they have entered into a relationship confident that any issues that may arise, if any, will resolve themselves without any help or work of their own. They assume that both people naturally have the same expectations and desires, arrogantly believing that their viewpoint is correct and that it is also the viewpoint of every other human being on earth. They are inundated with the way that their family of origin handles relationships, and more commonly, they are influenced by the broader culture, which is quicker to engage in premarital sex than it is to learn their partner's family history or even build relationships with their partner's family members.

After all, once sex becomes part of a relationship, it often takes the place of meaningful conversations, and partners may falsely assume their relationship is healthy simply because of their sexual involvement. This is why trust becomes so fragile in these situations. Both partners may genuinely believe they are progressing toward a more profound connection and commitment when, in reality, they are misreading the strength of their bond. Tovares Grey, co-author of *Godly Dating 101*, recounts a story about a friend of his who had a similar experience:

He genuinely thought the amount of sex they were having meant the relationship was healthy. How could she not truly love or respect him if they were always in bed together? But the problem with that mindset is that sex isn't a strong enough foundation to build a meaningful relationship on. Only Jesus is.

What many of us fail to realize is that sex outside of God's proper context, marriage, actually clouds our judgment. While we are thinking that this person surely must be the will of God for our lives, they are just a distraction. While we are on cloud nine and excited to be in a new relationship, it's really the orgasm that has blinded us to the fact that they have been pulling us away from our biblical convictions.

Premarital sex can create a false sense of security and intimacy, leading us to overlook potential red flags and deeper incompatibilities.

Among the many different expectations each person may have regarding specific roles and aspects of the day-to-day of the relationship, most have different expectations for the future. One partner may view premarital sex as a sign of a serious, long-term commitment, possibly leading to marriage. In contrast, the other might see it as part of a less defined or short-term relationship. When it becomes clear that both partners have differing expectations, feelings of betrayal and mistrust can arise. For instance, if one partner promises that the relationship is headed toward marriage and the other does not follow through, it can lead to a breakdown in trust.

Because it is more common for women to be the ones upholding a standard and commitment to abstinence until marriage, relationships often have the following pattern. The woman, who has communicated clearly and often to her male partner that she is unwilling to have sex until marriage, has established clear boundaries even though she is in a relationship with a man who does not share or hold her same convictions. He is attracted to the fact that he has found a "good girl" and recognizes the prize of what he has. Unfortunately, he is self-deceived. Though he is not manipulative or evil in the sense that he spends every day plotting how to convince his girlfriend to have sex with him, he is fully aware that the promise and future of marriage are something that she deeply desires. In her mind, because of the many relationships that she has been in in the past that have either not worked out or led to disappointment after she had already had sex, she views marriage as the ultimate security for the relationship.

Given that this relationship has at least discussed the topic of marriage, the longer they are together, the more lenient she becomes with her convictions. Feeling confident that this is the man that she will marry, she removes the boundaries of abstinence by convincing herself that this is my future husband who I will be with forever. The man views her also as his future wife and easily engages in premarital sex with his girlfriend. Due to the hormones released and the natural bond that sexual intimacy creates, their one-time sexual encounter becomes a continuous aspect of their relationship. They are now a loving couple that frequently engages in sex, and their convictions are nullified because they are convinced that they will be together forever. However, neither of these individuals knows their judgment has been compromised. And because they have entered into a premarital sexual relationship, the intentionality that they once had to get to know each other on a deeper level has been halted. Suddenly, they experience conflicts and miscommunication and even find themselves being severely jealous of one another. Suspicions arise that hurt their relationship as both of them feel a sense of entitlement to the other person and their body.

This world of muddy and complicated emotions that are only securely guarded in marriage quickly begins to unravel their once happy and future-facing relationship until neither can imagine a happy life together. The only two options left on the table are to ignore their conflict and emotions and get married simply because it was their original plan and promise to one another or to end the relationship because they are incompatible and cannot resolve their conflicts. As you can imagine, the correct solution is no longer obvious to them or us as observer simply because of how much premarital sex has complicated their relationship overall. And like many couples, this couple chooses to part ways, left with the baggage of another relationship where they engaged in premarital sex and bonded emotionally with a partner, only to break the bond that God never intended to be broken. Both of these individuals are completely unaware that the relationship has transformed them. It has not only warped their expectations but also made their hearts hard. They are now hardened toward the next individual they will enter into a relationship with and will now bring that same baggage from a previous relationship into another, unfairly tainting the next individual they decide to settle down with. This is the complex ripple effect that is set in motion when premarital sex is introduced, even with the best of intentions. This is a prime example of why premarital sex should be completely off the table for anyone who is seeking to honor God, their partner, and themselves. Their single decision to introduce and allow premarital sex into their relationship has now set a ripple effect into motion that will now follow them into every relationship they enter unless they decide to stand firmly on the conviction of abstinence and pursue a deep spiritual cleansing and heart change.

In addition to messes made by two people having two different expectations for the future, trust can be further eroded due to unfaithfulness or the entertaining of the emotional connection with others. This is likely to happen after premarital sex has been introduced due to the implicit or explicit promise of exclusivity that often accompanies a sexual relationship. The challenge arises because, without the covenant of marriage, the idea of exclusivity is not backed by any legal or covenantal

  Why men shouldn't have sex before marriage

mandate. This often leads to couples who engage in premarital sex feeling the liberty to remove their exclusivity at any moment of convenience that suits them best.

Another way trust can be eroded in a relationship that has premarital sex can be from inconsistent communication. When two individuals have a sexual relationship that is not sanctioned by the marriage covenant, it is easy for individuals to feel the pressure and expectation of communicating at a certain frequency and depth that has no clear boundaries. When this happens, one person who may feel like the person is only interested in them sexually and not available for them emotionally may begin to lose trust in their partner. They may feel used because their partner is not meeting their communication expectations, leading to insecurity.

Another example is that a person who was interested in marriage before sex was introduced may now change their mind and delay the idea of marriage after sex has been introduced. They may now say, "I'm not ready to rush into marriage just yet," which may be hurtful to the partner who believed that the sexual relationship was going to further secure their partner's commitment. This sending of mixed signals, especially if the sexual intimacy continues, causes great confusion and will only continue to erode trust over time.

One of the final examples that is important to bring up is a situation that I've often witnessed. I've known many couples who started their relationship off sexually and later became aware of how much their sexual intimacy was destroying their relationship spiritually and emotionally. These couples often decide to pursue abstinence and start the relationship off on a different foot. However, one of the challenges that often occurs is that a couple that has already begun their relationship with sexual intimacy on the table usually struggles deeply to build their relationship on an entirely new foundation. This is especially difficult when the foundation of their original relationship is as addictive and energizing as sex.

In most cases, one partner's commitment to pursue abstinence was stronger than the other person's. Yet, the other person agreed in order to appease the person they are in a relationship with. When the conviction is not shared equally and one hundred percent among both people, it is a recipe for disaster. In this instance, the partner who has set out to pursue abstinence may feel guilty for withholding sex from their partner who doesn't share the same commitment. When this happens, the partner who desires to pursue abstinence often gives in to their partner's temptations but then finds themselves in a cycle of guilt as they are torn between pursuing God or pleasing the partner they have invested so much time with.

It is indeed possible to have a relationship that is "all about sex." And especially if the sex is great, it is even more of a risk for the couple to completely abandon their emotional intimacy. Due to sexual intimacy releasing bonding hormones like oxytocin and vasopressin, couples may experience feelings of closeness and attachment while these chemical reactions mask their deeper emotional and relational issues. A couple may feel "connected" during or after sex but remain emotionally distant in other aspects of the relationship, such as communication or shared values. This can give the illusion of closeness, even when the foundation for a healthy, lasting relationship is weak.

With the prevalence of hook-up culture, there are also many couples that become emotionally bonded through sex so early in their relationship that they are completely unable to reason. And because they are sexually compatible and able to please one another, they falsely believe that they are soulmates. The worst thing happens when a couple makes this assumption and ignores all other aspects important to a relationship. They may rush to get married due to being disoriented in the fog of sexual intimacy. And this couple fast-tracks into a lifelong commitment only to discover that marriage requires much more than just a happy sex life.

In some cases, couples may use sex as a way to avoid addressing difficult emotional or relational issues. Rather than resolving conflicts or discussing important aspects of the relationship, the couple may turn to physical intimacy to "smooth things over." While this may create a temporary sense of closeness, it prevents deeper emotional connection from developing and can result in unresolved issues resurfacing later.

Some people falsely mistake sexual intimacy for the emotional intimacy that they are desperately in need of. These individuals often enter into relationships deeply wounded from past trauma or abuse. Research indicates that those who pursue sex in their relationships out of a desire to feel wanted, validated, and worthy are generally those who have been sexually abused. We will talk more about sexual abuse in a later chapter, but the warning is clear. Premarital sex often masks intimacy, falsely alluding to closeness and security that hasn't been cultivated or that has no chance of existing.

Another reason why premarital sex is harmful outside of marriage is because it may introduce conversations and topics that the couple has not established a proper level of safety and security in order to have productively.

Because every human desires to be deeply known and yet deeply loved, there is an innate desire to disclose what will most likely challenge our partner's devotion. We desire to be assured that the person we are with loves the real us, not just the version of us that we have portrayed or put forth for them to see. So in the case of premarital sex, responsible couples should be on the same page about each other's sexual health, family planning, and possibly even past sexual experiences. Because having sex can inevitably lead to infection and contraction of diseases, couples who are in a sexual relationship should be able to have a conversation about each other's sexual health without having the intimacy and the relationship as a whole put in jeopardy.

Likewise, couples should also be aware that having sex may lead to procreation and be able to have a mature and secure conversation about family planning and each other's desires or plans for children. They should also be able to have these conversations without fear of intimacy or the relationship being jeopardized. Lastly, individuals who are not virgins and who have the desire to build a relationship that is on a firm foundation of unconditional love should have the availability and opportunity to discuss their sexual past, no matter how dark or complicated it may be. Mature couples being able to discuss each other's sexual history is proof that they are committed to loving all of each other. Even perhaps the parts that are most difficult to accept or love. All of these are conversations that are immediately brought to the table in a sexual relationship.

Yet, unfortunately, culture has fed us the lie that we can have a sexual relationship without being honest or even addressing any of these things. The results are irresponsible, risky, and dangerous, negatively affecting both the partner's physical health and the relationship's communication and emotional dynamic. One of my favorite things about being married and having a sexual relationship with my wife is that we both have the opportunity to express our sexual expectations and desires openly and honestly without the fear that our relationship may be placed in jeopardy. Because my wife knows that I have proven I am committed to her and that I pledged my life to her without

 Why men shouldn't have sex before marriage

knowing her sexually, she knows that she can trust me with her sexual expectations or desires. And vice versa.

There is no fear of expressing my expectations or desires to my wife in my marriage. We have the opportunity to grow with one another each time we have sex by being able to be honest to share—what we liked, what we didn't like, what we want more of, what we would like to change—and all of this openness and honesty further enhances and helps us to develop a thriving sex life. I love knowing that if my wife tells me that she is not satisfied with my sexual performance, that does not mean that she will seek sexual fulfillment elsewhere. Instead, it means that she is telling me that she is not satisfied so that we can grow together until she is fully satisfied. This is the safety and security that is provided only when sex is reserved for marriage. No conversation is too difficult, and no conversation places our relationship at risk. We committed to love each other without ever knowing each other sexually, meaning that our relationship never has been and never will be based on sexual performance.

Imagine if we used the example of building a house to illustrate the concept of building a healthy relationship. We'll use the parts of the house to represent the many aspects of a relationship that are all important to longevity and success. The parts we'll focus on are the foundation, the walls, the roof, the windows and doors, and lastly the interior design. As you can imagine, some of these are more important than others and not all of them are necessary in order for the house to exist. Let's dive in and explore this illustration.

The foundation of the house represents the spiritual dimension of a relationship. Just as a house requires a stable foundation to remain upright and secure, a relationship thrives when grounded in shared spiritual beliefs and values. Spiritual connection provides the deepest sense of purpose and direction, offering strength during tough times. When a couple has a shared faith, they often find it easier to align their values and support each other through prayer, worship and shared moral principles. A solid spiritual foundation ensures the relationship is rooted in something greater than just the two individuals, allowing for long-term resilience.

The emotional dimension of a relationship can be likened to the walls of the house. Walls provide protection and structure, just as emotional intimacy creates a safe space for vulnerability and connection. Emotional walls represent the trust, understanding, and support that partners build between each other. The relationship is stable when the emotional walls are strong, providing security during life's storms. However, weak emotional walls—marked by unresolved conflicts or unaddressed emotional needs—can make the relationship unstable, just like cracks in the walls of a house can cause structural problems.

The roof represents the intellectual dimension of the relationship, offering coverage and protection, much like intellectual compatibility shields the relationship from misunderstandings or differences in worldview. Intellectual connection refers to shared interests, the ability to have meaningful conversations, and mutual respect for each other's thoughts and opinions. Just as a roof protects the house from external elements, intellectual compatibility ensures the couple can navigate life's challenges with understanding and shared problem-solving approaches. Without this, miscommunication or differing life perspectives can seep in like rain through a leaky roof.

The windows and doors of a house can represent communication within a relationship. Windows allow light to enter, and doors allow entry and exit, symbolizing openness, transparency, and access between partners. Effective communication lets fresh ideas, emotions, and perspectives flow freely, while

 Why men shouldn't have sex before marriage

poor communication keeps partners in the dark, leading to misunderstandings. Just as windows need to be cleaned regularly to let in light, communication in a relationship needs to be constantly maintained to ensure openness and clarity.

The physical dimension of a relationship can be likened to the interior design of a house. Just as interior design adds beauty and comfort to the home, physical intimacy can enhance closeness and connection in a relationship. However, much like how a home can exist and function without elaborate furnishings, a marriage can thrive even in the absence of sexual activity, mainly when spiritual, emotional, and intellectual bonds are strong. Couples who are physically or medically unable to engage in sexual intimacy can still have deeply fulfilling relationships because the core elements—spiritual foundation, emotional trust, and intellectual connection—are what hold the relationship together. This distinction is important because it shifts the focus from physical intimacy as the ultimate goal to a broader understanding of true relational intimacy. After all, the most relationally intimate man to walk the earth, Jesus Christ, lived his entire life unmarried, demonstrating that intimacy in relationships transcends physicality.

After discussing how premarital sex can erode trust and create a false sense of intimacy, it's essential to examine another layer of relationship dynamics—how withholding sexual involvement can reveal the true intentions and emotional maturity of a partner. When physical intimacy is delayed, a couple gains the opportunity to assess each other's values, communication skills, and long-term compatibility, which are often overshadowed by the emotional intensity of sex.

In *Boundaries in Dating*, Henry Cloud and John Townsend highlight the benefits of refraining from sex before marriage. They explain, "If you say no to sex outside of marriage, you will be able to discover a few crucial things while you are dating:

1. Does he or she want you for you, or just sex?

2. Is he or she capable of the other aspects of relating and intimacy, or has this person avoided developing those by just having sex? In other words, are you with an addict?

3. Is the person carrying around a lot of baggage inside that has never been healed?

4. Can this person delay gratification?

5. And, most importantly, does the person have the ability to submit to God?" (Cloud and Townsend, 2000, p. 254).

This excerpt supports the argument that premarital sex can obscure a clear understanding of a partner's character, motivations, and emotional health. By removing physical intimacy from the equation, both partners can focus on building a solid emotional, intellectual, and spiritual connection that serves as a stable foundation for a future together.

Moving forward, it's essential to explore how sexual involvement not only clouds relational judgment but can also affect personal goals and priorities. Premarital sex often leads to the prioritization of physical desires over long-term aspirations, causing shifts in focus that may hinder individual growth and derail the couple's shared objectives.

Many of us know people who entered relationships while thriving in their careers, supported by friends and family, and living with a clear sense of purpose. They were making great money, exercising influence, and fully focused on their mission in life. Yet, after starting a relationship that involves premarital sex, they seem to transform completely. This is more common than we think. The flood of hormones and chemical changes that occur during premarital sex can lead individuals to abandon their dreams, careers, and goals—things they have invested years of time, education, and resources in—just to prioritize the relationship.

Blinded by the emotional attachment that sex fosters, many of these individuals make impulsive decisions, such as moving in together, despite receiving strong advice against it from close friends or family members, whom they would normally heed if not so caught up in infatuation. In more extreme cases, they uproot their entire lives, moving far from their support system and often placing themselves in risky situations without much thought.

Another troubling pattern is the loss of individual identity. People who were once known for their unique convictions, creativity, or distinct personalities begin to conform to their partner's identity. This is particularly noticeable in individuals with strong beliefs or standout traits that once made them influential or impactful. They sacrifice their uniqueness, becoming a shadow of the person they once were, as they reshape their lives around the relationship. This is especially dangerous for men with a clear sense of mission and purpose. These men, who were once powerful influencers and seen as a threat to evil forces, can lose their spiritual edge and sense of calling due to the emotional entanglement of premarital sex.

As a Christian, I believe satan specifically targets men who have a sense of purpose, knowledge of their value, and who are a major threat to the kingdom of darkness. These men often throw away their future potential, and many never recover from the setback. They lose the relationship they've invested in and find themselves cut off from their previous life, distant from their support systems, and unable to regain the career success they once had. In the worst cases, they end up with children and ties to difficult partners, leaving them in complicated, unsupportive situations with no clear path forward.

In addition to the many ways that men sacrifice their future in the pursuit of relationships filled with premarital sex, many men also turn down significant life-altering and long-term opportunities. For example, suppose men are offered job promotions requiring them to relocate, receive scholarships to faraway schools, or any other promising opportunity. In that case, they may reject it because their relationship is more important. A study by the University of Arizona suggests that people may be willing to pass on career opportunities to maintain proximity to a romantic partner, reflecting how personal relationships can impact professional choices. This can lead to stunted career growth or missed opportunities, affecting their long-term financial and professional trajectory.

Sexual relationships can also cause people to modify or limit their social interactions. The desire to spend more time with a romantic partner, coupled with the emotional bonds created by sex, can lead to the gradual distancing from friends, family, or other social networks. A strong sexual attachment may cause individuals to disregard advice from close friends or family members, who might see warning signs in the relationship that the involved person is too emotionally compromised to recognize. This social isolation can leave individuals without a robust support system, which they might need later if the relationship deteriorates.

Over time, people who continually engage in premarital sex may feel guilt, shame, or diminished self-worth. These emotional responses can shape how individuals see themselves and their future decisions. People may develop a sense of inadequacy or feel that they no longer meet the standards they once held for themselves, impacting their confidence in other areas of life.

While we explored extensively the ways premarital sex affects our romantic and marital relationships, there are several ways that it harms our platonic relationships with friends and family as well. Engaging in premarital sex can affect our relationship with friends by forcing us to become distanced from them as we begin to spend more and more time with our partner. It can also lead to individuals becoming more secretive or guarded from friends with whom they usually would have a layer of trust and vulnerability. This is especially the case if these individuals feel shame, guilt, or a desire to hide their actions from their close friends or social circle to maintain their approval. Premarital sex can have a similar negative effect on family relationships. It may lead to tension, particularly in cultures or communities where abstinence until marriage is highly valued. If a person engages in premarital sex against the values of their family, this can cause feelings of disappointment and strain or even lead to conflict.

According to research conducted by the Greater Good Science Center at UC Berkeley, individuals with multiple sexual partners before marriage are more likely to report lower satisfaction in their future relationships. A scenario comparing two individuals, one with multiple partners and one with only their spouse, illustrates how past sexual experiences may lead to unrealistic comparisons in marriage. This comparison increases the likelihood of dissatisfaction due to idealized memories of previous sexual experiences. One significant effect of premarital sex is the formation of a baseline of sexual pleasure, intimacy, and emotional connection that individuals may compare to future partners. These comparisons can lead to dissatisfaction if new partners do not meet or exceed previous experiences, undermining emotional and relational commitment.

In chapter 9 of my first book, "If Jesus Was a Rapper," I spoke about how both me and my wife met each other still having sexual pasts that we needed to be healed and purged of. We were deeply aware that even though we were virgins towards one another, our previous sexual experiences could create a wedge between us. This wedge could cause us to compare each other to previous sexual partners, prevent us from appreciating one another, and interrupt our intimacy by flooding our minds with memories of people from our past. As I wrote in that book, "Doing the difficult work of removing your previous sexual experiences and washing your mind and heart can only be done with God and His Word. Removing these thoughts would allow our sex life to be as if it were our first time —renewed virgins who knew no one but each other."

When the LORD placed this on my heart, I and Denya were new to our dating relationship. We were far from being engaged and even further from being married. But we were two Christians who understood the purpose of dating and who were intentionally preparing for marriage. This meant that every date and moment we spent together was filled with meaningful conversations about getting to know each other. It didn't take long for us to sense that we didn't know much about each other. Because there was so much we still didn't know, we never said: "I love you." We know how many people lie and jump into relationships, throwing these words around when all they know is the good things the person put forth for them to see. You don't truly love a person until you know the unloveable things about them and yet still choose to commit to them. By God's grace, we understood this and knew it was a lie to say we loved each other. We deeply liked what we had uncovered so far but knew the test of love was still waiting for us.

Through countless dates of creating safe spaces, listening to each other, and learning as much about each other as possible, I sensed the LORD leading us to a moment of transparency. We knew this moment would be the test of whether we truly loved each other, so we scheduled an intimate date where we would talk about our sexual past, wounds, and all the other uncomfortable things that neither one of us would ever discover unless it was shared. This was the scariest moment of our lives, as we knew everything we shared would be the very things that would make most people run away. We knew that we could make it through anything if we walked away from that conversation and committed to each other. And though what we uncovered that day hurt us and made us count the cost, we now had all the information we needed to make a prayerful decision about whether we should be together.

That conversation changed us forever, as it was our first moment of realizing the cost of loving one another. It was also one of the moments when I witnessed the Holy Spirit inside of Denya and His empowering her to be bold, transparent, and unashamed of where God had brought her from. Others who were not committed to Jesus would've denied my request for us to be transparent about our sexual histories and would've ended the relationship the moment I abandoned the feel-good and surface level. That day, Denya and I proved we were committed to honesty, transparency, and, most importantly, Jesus Christ. Our knowledge of how much Jesus loved us produced a freedom that made rejection from one another secondary. And while I understand that our method may not work for every couple, it has been the solid foundation for our trust and emotional compatibility. Our marriage and sex life are thriving today because of our difficult conversations while dating.

Lichter, Turner, and Sassler's findings for Social Science Research about cohabitation also highlight some powerful truths about couples who move in together before marriage. Their 2010 study highlights that individuals who engage in serial cohabitation are more likely to experience marital instability and also have higher marital dissolution. This is further proof of how cohabitation and multiple sexual relationships can contribute to long-term relationship challenges. Moreover, psychological studies suggest that individuals who engage in premarital sex may develop attachment insecurities, which can affect trust and emotional intimacy in future relationships. These insecurities may manifest as fears of inadequacy or jealousy, particularly if partners have different sexual histories.

Previous sexual relationships can also introduce trust issues, particularly if infidelity or betrayal occurred in past encounters. This can lead to heightened insecurity and fear within marriage, making it harder to form a stable and trusting bond. For instance, research by the Institute for Family Studies highlights that individuals with higher numbers of sexual partners before marriage often report more difficulties in maintaining trust and security in their marriages. There is a concept referred to as "sexual imprinting," where individuals subconsciously attach emotional significance to their first few sexual partners. Sexual imprinting can make it difficult to fully commit to a spouse later on. The emotional residue from these past relationships may prevent the individual from fully investing in their marriage, leading to less commitment and an increased risk of divorce. This is corroborated by studies indicating that individuals who have had numerous premarital sexual relationships are more likely to struggle with marital commitment.

Out of the men I interviewed for the writing of this book, all of the men who remained virgins until they were married expressed high marital satisfaction. On a scale of 1-10, with ten being the highest, all their rankings fell between 8-10. They expressed deep fulfillment in their marriages, while the men I interviewed who had not remained virgins ranked their marital satisfaction as low as 5. The men who remained virgins were also overwhelmingly more satisfied sexually in their marriages than the men who had not remained virgins. Many of them expressed that this was the case because their partners were the only sexual experience they had, automatically being the best sexual experience they had. It was also worth noting that no men who had remained virgins until marriage regretted their decisions or struggled to discuss with their spouse their particular sexual needs or desires.

Your desire to have sex might leave you like it did Keenan. Here's Keenan story:

Keenan had finally moved to Texas, hoping for a fresh start. Growing up in a rough urban neighborhood, he had always fallen in with the wrong crowd—constantly surrounded by drugs, crime, and a lifestyle fueled by unhealthy habits. After multiple stints in a rehabilitation program for his drug addiction and consistent spiritual support, Keenan was ready to leave his old life behind. Texas represented a new beginning, where he wouldn't have to deal with the negative peer pressure that had defined his past. He enrolled in a local community college and found a part-time job to pay for his apartment and car, working hard to build a more stable and fulfilling life.

A few months into his new chapter, Keenan met a woman named Layla, and they quickly started dating. Their relationship soon became physical, and Keenan moved in with her and her two children when his finances became tight. Overnight, he found himself not only as a boyfriend but also as a stepfather, taking on responsibilities he hadn't anticipated, including helping support her kids financially.

However, the premarital sexual relationship had brought on a storm of emotions that Keenan wasn't prepared for. He and Layla started having frequent arguments, often escalating into physical altercations. Whenever things got heated, Layla would call the police, and Keenan would end up in jail. This destructive cycle derailed his efforts to build a stable life. Every time he found a new part-time job and saved money, another conflict would arise, landing him back in jail and getting him fired. This left him perpetually starting over from scratch.

The rocky relationship with Layla didn't just affect his finances. It also disrupted his schooling, causing him to miss classes and withdraw frequently, wasting his time and money and preventing him from making any real progress toward his long-term goals. Every time Keenan tried to regain his footing, the emotional baggage of the relationship would pull him back down.

Whenever Keenan and I speak, he talks about how trapped he feels, stuck between his love for Layla and her children and the increasingly clear realization that their toxic relationship is holding him back. Despite his desire for stability, he can't escape the cycle of conflict and codependency. His biggest revelation has been that premarital sex has been at the heart of his struggles in every phase of his life. It isn't just the external environment or the people around him leading him astray—it is his unchecked desires and lack of self-discipline.

The story of Keenan and Layla illustrates how premarital sex can have ripple effects that extend far beyond the immediate relationship. As discussed throughout this chapter, the act of engaging in sex outside of marriage often sets off a chain of emotional, relational, and psychological consequences that can affect trust, communication, and intimacy. When disrupted early on, these dynamics create a fragile foundation, leading to long-term relational instability. The patterns seen in their story, such as codependency and emotional volatility, are not isolated events but part of a broader picture that highlights how premarital sex can lead individuals to compromise on their life goals and priorities, sometimes even stalling personal growth and future aspirations.

 Why men shouldn't have sex before marriage

Beyond the short-term consequences, these experiences can profoundly shape one's sense of self-worth and identity, as people may carry unaddressed emotional baggage into future relationships, hindering their chances of building healthy families. As seen with Keenan and Layla, the presence of violence in their relationship is not uncommon when sexual boundaries are crossed prematurely. This chapter only scratched the surface of how sexual dynamics can fuel negative behaviors, but in the next chapter, we will explore a deeper connection between premarital sex and sexual violence. The patterns of control, power struggles, and manipulation often found in such relationships will be examined more closely, revealing how sexual choices can set the stage for even darker realities.

CHAPTER 3:

The Dark Side of Premarital Sex

Sexual activity, in its healthiest and most sacred form, is designed to occur within the covenant of marriage between a man and a woman. This is not only a spiritual belief but a conviction grounded in the understanding that marriage provides the framework of commitment, trust, and mutual respect necessary to safeguard both partners. Any sexual act outside of this marital bond—whether it's between two unmarried adults, with underage children, or involving vulnerable individuals—is a violation of the very sanctity that protects the integrity of sexual relationships.

When society engages in premarital sex, it opens the door to a host of negative consequences, not just for those directly involved but also for the broader culture, where sexual exploitation and abuse thrive. The normalization of sex outside of marriage can weaken the boundaries meant to protect individuals from manipulation, coercion, and violence. Without the guardrails of a monogamous marital relationship, sexual activity becomes disconnected from its purpose, increasing the likelihood of abuse.

The solution is straightforward: by returning to the belief that sexual activity belongs solely within marriage, we can create a culture that prioritizes safety, consent, and respect. Those who choose to embrace this solution will not only protect themselves from the harmful effects of premarital sex but also contribute to reducing the prevalence of sexual abuse in all its forms. Though this view may not be universally accepted, it remains an essential step in preventing the cycle of exploitation that results when sex is detached from commitment and responsibility. This chapter will explore the link between premarital sex and sexual violence, demonstrating how the erosion of sexual boundaries facilitates abuse and why abstinence before marriage is a critical factor in stopping it.

Marital rape is a terrible reality, and I'm incredibly sad that it occurs. I have so much respect for those who have survived marital rape and would never want to minimize their experiences or suggest that marriage is a blanket protection against abuse. While marital rape does occur, it is far less common than some critics of marriage would have us believe. And even in those cases where marital rape does occur, few of those cases exist among couples who were both virgins when they got married. This is because abstinence is the best protection against sexual violence. The solution lies in fostering a culture of mutual respect and consent within marriage. Abstinence before marriage can help set the stage for marriages where both partners are committed to trust, respect, and equality—key factors in preventing sexual violence within marriages.

While this book specifically targets men, I have chosen to address men based purely on science. Let me be clear and say that I do not believe men are superior to women in any way and that my argument is purely based on historical and sociological trends. Research and history confirm that the direction in which society moves has always been in response to men's leadership. When men lose value in marriage, women also lose value. And when men prioritize their families, women also prioritize their families. Controversial or not, it's the truth. And it's a picture of the influence and dominion that God gave to men. Our job is to lead by example because—what men do, women do. A big reason for the massive decline in healthy marriages and a major increase in sexual violence is that men have abandoned abstinence. Encouraging men to embrace abstinence and healthy marital relationships isn't about placing all the responsibility on men, but rather recognizing our societal impact and leadership potential. Empowering men to lead responsibly is a path toward healthier relationships for all.

Research shows that most perpetrators of sexual violence and abuse are victims themselves. This means that somewhere in our psyche of being hurt and never wanting to repeat the atrocities committed against us, we become the very monsters we despise. The person who forced us to be the object of their sexual gratification violated the mandate to save all sexual activity for marriage. A child's innocence wouldn't have been lost if they had followed this rule.

I'm sure people are reading this saying, "It's not that simple." "Not everyone is married or ever will be." "Premarital sex doesn't directly cause sexual violence." "What about the social and psychological factors that lead to abuse?" "What about consent?" And "not everyone believes in marriage or even wants to wait." I hear you, validate you, and want to address your thoughts.

First off, while premarital sex itself may not directly cause sexual violence, it can contribute to a culture that normalizes non-committed sexual relationships, reducing the societal emphasis on respect, consent, and emotional responsibility. This erosion of boundaries creates an environment where sexual exploitation and coercion are more likely. In this way, promoting abstinence can help reinforce a cultural norm that prioritizes commitment and respect, reducing the likelihood of such abuse.

Secondly, it is essential to acknowledge that sexual abuse often has roots in issues like power, control, trauma, and mental health. For example, child abuse, domestic violence, and trauma are often linked to systemic issues rather than premarital sexual activity alone. I'm arguing that abstinence before marriage creates an environment where sex is valued as part of a larger commitment, encouraging individuals to address emotional and psychological needs in healthier ways. Premarital sex can contribute to a cycle of casual relationships and emotional instability, which can lead to exploitation or abusive situations. I believe that abstinence, combined with a focus on healthy, committed relationships, offers a pathway to emotional and relational stability.

Thirdly, while I believe that sex should be reserved for a married heterosexual relationship between a man and woman, still I think this book has tremendous value for any reader, even those who don't identify as heterosexual. I also am aware that limiting sexual activity to heterosexual marriage doesn't necessarily prevent sexual violence in non-heterosexual contexts. However, the core of my argument is about the importance of commitment, respect, and mutual care in sexual relationships. All readers should be able to appreciate my argument that sex outside of a committed, monogamous relationship can lead to exploitation and harm.

And lastly, I am not attempting to overlook the role consent plays in reducing sexual violence. Instead, I am seeking to emphasize that abstinence before marriage is not just about avoiding sex, but about creating a culture of respect, communication, and consent that carries over into marriage. The commitment of marriage naturally fosters these values, and abstinence can be a way of preparing for a relationship where mutual respect and clear boundaries are prioritized. Thus, abstinence is a proactive way to prevent situations where consent may be compromised.

When God created sex, He intended it to be glorious, beautiful, and an act of worship unto Him. We know this is true because it was explicitly given and reserved for the covenant of marriage as a means of physical pleasure and enjoyment as well as procreation. The physical enjoyment piece was there to bond two married individuals in the closest form of physical intimacy that exists and also as a way to procreate and produce children that would continuously wreak havoc on the kingdom of darkness. This is why the Old Testament is filled with reminders for God's followers to share their testimonies of God's faithfulness and who God is to their children's children and any generations that follow. The Bible is very clear that every future generation that comes to know God is a win for the kingdom and that the task of taking dominion over the earth and subduing it can only come through flooding the world with other human beings who have the heart of God and who understand their missional purpose as well.

In sex, the moment of climax and orgasm may be single-handedly one of the most heavenly moments that exists on earth. To orgasm can be understood as an out-of-body experience connecting us to an extreme euphoria that can only be similar to the euphoria that we will experience eternally at the feet of

Jesus. It doesn't take a rocket scientist to make the connection that this incredible feeling of orgasm, euphoria, and taste of heaven is what all of humanity has been on a constant search for—and addicted to. People in every situation and since the beginning of time have pursued the high of sexual orgasm even at the expense of seeking it outside of the original relationship for which the Lord intended it. Similarly to what happened in the garden with Adam and Eve and the serpent in Genesis chapter 3, our world has looked at sex (which God created) and incorrectly assumed that if God does not want me to have this, then he must not be a good God and He must be keeping things from me. This is the same heart that Adam and Eve had in the garden when they wrongfully assumed that God must not love them or want them to enjoy their life because He had given them boundaries about which tree and fruit they were not to partake of.

Because we've done the same thing with sex, it has been easy for the serpent to deceive us with the lie that God does not want us to be happy or sexually fulfilled. Because we are detached from the heart of God, many of us have misunderstood His laws as burdensome instead of recognizing the ways they protect us. Every law or boundary God places on humanity and His people is always there to guide them to the fullest experience of the life He has given them. As the scripture says in John 10:10, "The thief comes only to steal and kill and destroy. I came that they may have life and have it abundantly. (ESV)" Because the heart of God is that we would have an abundant and fulfilled life, it cannot be true that God has decided to withhold sex from us. Instead, it must be true that there are dangers if we ignore God's boundaries and pursue sex on our own terms. In addition to the adverse effects of premarital sex, which we've already uncovered in the first two chapters of this book, one of the significant things that I believe the Lord is seeking to protect us from is sexual violence and abuse.

When premarital sex becomes normalized, it can blur the lines of what constitutes consent. In a culture where casual hookups or fleeting sexual encounters are accepted, the expectation for clear, enthusiastic consent can become muddied. This normalization may lead to scenarios where consent is assumed or coerced rather than explicitly sought. A study by Jozkowski and Peterson titled *"College Students and Sexual Consent: Unique Insights"* was published in the *Journal of Sex Research* in 2013. The research showed that in casual or non-committed sexual relationships, the clarity around consent can become blurred due to pressures and expectations surrounding sexual activity. This study on college students suggests that individuals in non-committed relationships often experience difficulty in communicating sexual consent, as they may feel pressured to conform to the sexual expectations of their partner. This can lead to situations where consent is not clearly established or respected, increasing the risk of boundary violations. Additionally, non-verbal cues and assumptions based on prior sexual activity can further complicate consent in these scenarios.

Furthermore, this study highlights that individuals who frequently engage in casual sex may become desensitized to the importance of consent, which erodes the distinction between consensual and non-consensual encounters. This pressure to meet perceived sexual norms or expectations often reduces the ability to assert boundaries, especially when emotional intimacy or trust is lacking. Jozkowski and Peterson showed that people engaging in casual sexual encounters are more likely to face situations where boundaries are crossed, particularly in relationships that lack long-term commitment or trust. This is often linked to the more fluid nature of casual relationships, where expectations around exclusivity and emotional attachment can be less clear compared to committed, long-term partnerships.

The fact that many of these relationships are centered more on physical gratification than an emotional connection is the perfect breeding ground for abuse.

Here's a simple illustration to help understand how consent can become muddied using two nineteen year old college students who have been dating for a few weeks.

One night, Malik and Sofia are at a party. They've had fun hanging out, laughing, and dancing. As the night winds down, Malik asks Sofia if she wants to go back to his dorm. Sofia agrees to go, thinking they will just hang out and talk like usual.

When they arrive, Malik makes some jokes about how they've been dating for a while, and he starts hinting at how "most couples do more than just talk." He feels like he's put in the time by taking Sofia on dates, and now he expects things to move to a more physical level. From Malik's perspective, he's invested in this relationship, and he believes that he's "earned" something in return. In his mind, this isn't anything wrong—he's just doing what he thinks is normal for relationships at their stage.

Sofia, however, feels a bit pressured. She likes Malik and doesn't want to disappoint him, but she's not quite ready to go as far as he wants. She feels that maybe she "owes" him something because he's been so nice to her, but deep down, she doesn't feel entirely comfortable.

Malik doesn't see the situation from Sofia's perspective. For him, consent has become something like a transaction—a silent deal where time, attention, and effort on his part should naturally lead to physical intimacy. He assumes that since Sofia hasn't directly said no, she's okay with it, but he doesn't realize that real consent means making sure both people are on the same page, with no pressure involved.

This illustration is just an example of how consent can become transactional and how premarital sex can unknowingly become abuse. Another layer that I would like to bring up is called desensitization to exploitation. This is when media and culture inundate us with casual sex so much that we began to believe that everyone we meet is comfortable with casual sex. The dangers of this are obvious and are sustained by both men and women being indoctrinated with complimentary lies. Men are being told that "if a girl is alone with you, she wants to have sex", and women are being told "it's not sexy or attractive to appear opposed to sex when a man desires it". Both of these lies perpetuate a culture that is harmful and abusive. Here's a simple illustration to help us understand desensitization to exploitation.

Andre and Nia meet through mutual friends and quickly start hanging out. Both are influenced by the shows they watch, where casual sex is often portrayed as no big deal. Andre's favorite show frequently depicts guys hooking up with women without much conversation or emotional connection. Nia has noticed how the female characters in her favorite show are praised for being "confident" when they have casual relationships.

One night, Andre and Nia end up alone together after a party. They've been flirting for weeks, and Andre starts to move toward being more intimate. Nia hesitates but remembers how women on her favorite show always go along with the moment and seem to enjoy it. She tells herself that it's "just what people do" and pushes her discomfort aside.

On the other hand, Andre has seen countless scenes in movies and TV where guys who persist eventually get what they want. In his mind, he's not being manipulative—he's just playing the game the way it's always been shown. He doesn't recognize that Nia is uncomfortable because he's been desensitized by the

 Why men shouldn't have sex before marriage

media he consumes. For him, the lines of what's consensual and what's coercive have blurred.

As their encounter continues, Nia feels like she has to go along with it, even though she's not truly comfortable. Andre assumes she's on board because she didn't stop him. Neither of them realizes that their understanding of consent and exploitation has been skewed by the media's glorification of casual sex, where boundaries are often ignored or trivialized. This illustration is an example of how the media we consume influences how we think about sex. It also highlights how the media we consume also builds our framework for how we believe others feel and experience sex—both of which are generally problematic based on society's trends. In chapter seven, we'll discuss media, its influences, and the importance of filtering the content we consume.

As the earlier research indicated, individuals who engage in premarital sex more often have a higher chance of experiencing a situation where boundaries are crossed. This happens because many men mistakenly believe that if a girl has given consent to sex in the past, she automatically agrees to future sexual encounters. This mindset and popular way of thinking further highlights the lack of commitment, respect, and trust associated with premarital sex. Without the framework of marriage, where trust and mutual respect are foundational, sexual activity may be subject to inaccurate assumptions and occur in contexts where power imbalances or manipulative behaviors are more likely to surface. This is another reason why premarital sex further increases the risk of violence or coercion.

The media, mainly through TV, movies, and music, often portrays casual sex as fun, consequence-free, and a normal part of everyday life. This contributes to a broader cultural acceptance of premarital sex and may diminish the perceived significance of consent and boundaries. Moreover, the pervasive influence of pornography, which often portrays aggressive or non-consensual behavior as erotic, further distorts societal views on sexual relationships and boundaries.

As a pastoral counselor and staff member at a church, I often would speak to women who were survivors of sexual abuse. In many cases, as research supports, their abusers were often close family members, uncles, or their mom's boyfriends. These stories and realities are always sad because they directly speak to the damage caused by sexual activity outside of a healthy marriage. In these conversations, I'd often ask these women whether they believe the sexual abuse they endured would've still occurred had their biological fathers been present in the home. In all of the cases I've encountered, each woman answered "No". They overwhelmingly were confident that their father not being present left them vulnerable to abuse. These responses, which I eventually began to anticipate, forced me to recognize and realize the importance of men being in committed marriages and choosing not to have premarital sex.

The cycle and web of consequences around premarital sex remain deeply intertwined, as premarital sex continues to be a common factor in numerous cases of abuse and exploitation. When men engage in premarital sex, leading to unplanned pregnancies, many feel unprepared for fatherhood, which often results in pressure on the mother to seek an abortion. In situations where the mother chooses to keep the child, many men choose to leave, leading to fatherless households and leaving mothers to raise children without a supportive father figure. This family disruption has widespread effects, including an increased risk of child abuse.

Research reveals that family disruption, especially in female-headed, single-parent households, is one of the greatest risk

 Why men shouldn't have sex before marriage

factors for child abuse, with approximately 43 percent of children in such homes reported as abuse victims in 1981. This 1981 statistic may seem outdated, but it is a benchmark illustrating an alarming trend that has only intensified over time. Since the 1960s, fatherlessness, premarital sex, and abuse rates have surged even higher, meaning the impact today is likely even more severe. The likelihood of sexual abuse triples when a father is absent from the home, exposing children to heightened vulnerabilities. Fatherlessness, research shows, is closely related to issues like delinquency, premature sexuality, and even crime. In fact, about 60 percent of rapists, 72 percent of adolescent murderers, and 70 percent of long-term prison inmates come from fatherless homes, underscoring the crucial role of fathers in shaping self-control, empathy, and discipline in their children.

Research also indicates that children raised without fathers are significantly more likely to engage in premarital sex, and this trend leads to broader, generational impacts. Between 1960 and 1990 alone, the percentage of children living apart from their biological fathers more than doubled from 17 percent to 36 percent, revealing a sharp decline in fatherhood and family stability. The consequences of this decline reach deep into society, as Popenoe's findings highlight: fatherlessness fuels numerous societal problems, including crime, adolescent delinquency, early sexual activity, educational challenges, and even poverty. While multiple factors contribute to these issues, the presence of a father consistently serves as a protective factor. For example, a father's presence is shown to deter premature sexual activity in children and significantly reduce their chances of being victimized by sexual abuse.

In addition to individual impacts, research shows that communities with strong family structures and norms around marriage generally report lower rates of sexual exploitation and abuse. These structures provide clear expectations for responsible behavior, which strengthen social bonds and personal accountability. However, when sexual norms break down, the larger social structure weakens in turn. As sex becomes detached from the context of marriage, it becomes more commodified and transactional, diminishing its inherent value. In these casual encounters, individuals often see each other not as people worthy of respect but as objects for sexual gratification. This objectification contributes to exploitation, where one party may feel entitled to another's body without considering emotional or ethical boundaries. Furthermore, studies like Kathleen Kiernan's National Child Development Study analysis show that young women from disrupted families—especially those with divorced or separated parents—tend to engage in premarital sex and bear children outside of marriage, often repeating the cycle of unstable family structures.

The connection between fatherlessness and the cycle of exploitation and abuse is profound, as a father's absence leaves children both unsupervised and emotionally deprived, making them more susceptible to abusers who exploit their need for affection, attention, and guidance. Even well-meaning absent fathers cannot provide the same level of protection or form the close emotional bonds that in-home fathers can. Research emphasizes that girls in fatherless homes, in particular, are at risk; for instance, approximately one in six women with a stepfather experiences abuse compared to one in 40 with a biological father. This sobering data reveals how crucial an intact family and fatherly presence are in fostering a safer, more stable environment for children.

In light of this, it is essential for men to remain abstinent until marriage, prioritizing stable, committed relationships not only for their own well-being but for that of future generations.

The ripple effect of this decision reaches far beyond immediate satisfaction; it lays a foundation for communities built on mutual respect, safety, and dignity.

If you are reading all of this about the prevalence of abuse and how premarital sex creates more opportunities for abuse to occur, you may be wondering what allows these situations to happen so frequently. To answer this question, it is important to recognize what professionals have discovered about premarital sex and the circumstances that often surround it. Research into the dynamics of abusive relationships frequently highlights how vulnerable individuals—such as younger partners, economically dependent individuals, or emotionally vulnerable people—are exploited by those with more power. Premarital and casual sex often occur in relationships with significant power imbalances— whether economic, emotional, or age-related. Without the ethical framework that marital norms often provide, individuals in positions of power may exploit the vulnerability of others, leading to situations of manipulation or abuse. Additionally, a 2019 study examining how men and women communicate (or often fail to communicate) before sexual encounters found that both genders culturally believed sex was meant to "just happen" without direct communication, often relying instead on perceived body language cues. Participants indicated that less verbal communication enhanced sexual chemistry, but this lack of clarity blurred the lines between consent and assumption, often leaving consent unspoken and assumed rather than explicitly given.

Power dynamics in these encounters further complicate consent. The same study revealed that men often sought out women who appeared more sexually provocative, while women gravitated toward men who played "hard to get." This unspoken pattern placed men in the role of "conqueror" and women as "hint-givers," reinforcing underlying power structures where men are seen as initiators, pursuing "seductive" women who appear passive but receptive. This dynamic can facilitate manipulation, as the lack of open communication paired with established roles leaves room for misinterpretation and exploitation. Further, older men were often considered desirable by women for their perceived maturity, stability, and strength, creating another layer of power imbalance in such relationships. This research confirms the complex ways unspoken consent, societal power structures, and the absence of clear communication contribute to blurred boundaries and the potential for abuse. As the weakening of sexual norms continues, it allows predators to rationalize exploitation as part of an assumed "freedom," further compromising the safety and autonomy of vulnerable individuals.

I must provide clear definitions when introducing the idea of vulnerable individuals or populations. When I speak of vulnerable individuals or populations, I mean the following. Certain groups are more susceptible to exploitation, including young people, economically disadvantaged individuals, and those with limited access to education. These populations often lack the resources or agency to assert their autonomy in sexual situations. Research highlights that young women, in particular, are vulnerable to coercion in premarital relationships, especially when societal norms glorify casual sex or when they experience peer pressure to conform to sexually permissive cultures. Here's an illustration of how age can be a contributor to power imbalances in sexual relationships:

A younger woman who is dating an older man may be more at risk of being taken advantage of because she might not have as much life experience or confidence as him. The older guy might know more about relationships and use that to pressure her into doing things she isn't ready for. Since she may not feel as sure about setting boundaries, it's easier for him to take control or convince her to go along with his wishes. This can make her more likely to be in an unhealthy or abusive situation, even if she doesn't realize it right away.

There is also the reality of increased coercion in non-committed relationships. The absence of long-term commitment in non-marital or casual sexual encounters often creates an environment ripe for exploitation. In these settings, individuals may feel pressured to engage in sexual activity to maintain their relationship or avoid conflict, especially if they believe sex is expected as part of the exchange in the relationship. Here's an illustration of how the desire to maintain friendship or relationship can lead to exploitation and coercion:

In a "friends with benefits" relationship, one person might feel pressured to keep having sex because they worry that if they don't, the friendship or special connection could end. For example, if one friend starts wanting more emotional support or closeness, they might feel like they have to go along with sexual activity just to keep the other person around. They might think that saying no could make things awkward or cause the relationship to fall apart. This creates a situation where they feel forced to do something they don't really want to, just to keep the peace or maintain the friendship.

The reality of exploitation is also connected to economic or social power imbalances. Research has shown that individuals in precarious financial situations or with less social capital are more likely to be exploited or coerced into sex. For example, when one partner is financially dependent on the other, they may feel compelled to engage in sexual activity against their will. Here's an illustration of how economic imbalances can result in "survival sex":

Tasha had been couch-surfing for months, her clothes stuffed into a single backpack, and she was always worried about where she'd sleep next. Then she met Jay, an older guy with his own place, who offered her a room. At first, he seemed kind—he bought her dinner and let her stay the night without asking for anything. But soon, Jay made it clear that if Tasha wanted to keep staying with him, she'd have to "give something back." Tasha knew what he meant. She didn't want to sleep with him, but the thought of being back on the streets with no food or shelter scared her more than anything. So, she told herself it wasn't that bad—a warm bed, food, and safety, all for a little bit of herself in return. It didn't feel right, but it seemed like the only option in her mind.

Media and culture have also promoted "hookup culture," which comes with its own set of hidden expectations and pressures. "Hookup culture" leaves many individuals feeling desensitized to coercion, as they may internalize the expectation that sexual activity is part of any relationship, whether they desire it or not. Research from the Journal of Sex Research points to the increased occurrence of sexual coercion in hookup cultures, especially in college settings. Many individuals, especially women, report feeling pressure to engage in sexual activities they were not entirely comfortable with due to peer expectations, alcohol use, and ambiguous boundaries within casual relationships. Here's an illustration of how "hookup culture" creates a landscape where sexual boundaries are increasingly blurred, and the line between consensual sex and exploitation becomes less clear:

Leah and Mike met at a party, and both were already a little tipsy when they started talking. The loud music and dim lights made it easy to forget their nerves. Without even discussing it, they both reached for more drinks, knowing that alcohol would make everything simpler. The buzz made Leah feel less shy, and

Mike felt like he could move things along faster. Later, they ended up back at Mike's apartment. Neither of them had really talked about what they wanted, but the alcohol blurred the lines. When Mike made a move, Leah hesitated for a moment but felt like she'd gone too far to say no now. She didn't want to come off as "difficult" or "awkward," and besides, all her friends had told her that hooking up was just part of college life. Mike, on the other hand, assumed Leah was fine with everything because she hadn't objected, even though deep down, both of them knew they were using the alcohol to push past any lingering doubts. The next morning, Mike couldn't shake the feeling that maybe Leah hadn't been as ready as he thought.

In addition to culture's normalization of sex, many people fail to realize the psychological effects that are a result of coerced sexual relationships. Victims often experience guilt, shame, or confusion about their sexual experiences, making it difficult for them to establish healthy boundaries in future relationships. This emotional damage can perpetuate a cycle of exploitation, where individuals who have been exploited in the past are more likely to experience similar situations again. Here's an illustration detailing this psychological trauma:

Jason had been in a relationship where his girlfriend constantly pressured him to have sex, even when he didn't feel ready or comfortable. She would say things like, "You're a man; you should want this," and he'd feel guilty if he didn't go along with it. Over time, he started to believe that sex was the only way to prove himself in a relationship. Now, in a new relationship, Jason feels conflicted. Even when his current girlfriend says she's not ready for physical intimacy, he struggles with his own instincts, thinking he's supposed to push things forward to avoid being rejected again. His judgment feels off, and he's confused about what a healthy relationship should look like. The pressure and guilt from his past relationship make it hard for him to trust his own feelings and respect boundaries, leaving him questioning whether his actions are ever truly respectful or just a reaction to what he's been through.

In all the illustrations and examples I've included above, research clearly indicates that premarital sexual activity can increase vulnerability to exploitation and coercion—particularly among populations with fewer resources or weaker social protections. By understanding how casual sexual relationships, power imbalances, and the cultural normalization of sex outside marriage contribute to exploitation, we can better address these challenges and advocate for healthier sexual norms that prioritize respect, consent, and equality in intimate relationships.

It is important to understand the psychological and societal impacts that result from sex being removed from a commitment-centered framework. For men, detaching sex from commitment may lead to difficulty forming deep, meaningful relationships later. Repeated casual experiences can numb emotional sensitivity, leading to desensitization and making it harder to cultivate emotional intimacy with your future spouse. This can also result in a "transactional" view of sex, where the act is seen more as a physical exchange rather than an emotional bond. Over time, this can warp perceptions of healthy relationships and distort the purpose of mutual respect and partnership.

One man that I interviewed while writing this book shared with me about the realities of becoming desensitized and numb to the emotional aspects of sex. Before he encountered Jesus and was radically transformed, his transactional view of sex resulted in him having sex with more than 100 women. He spoke about the damage of that lifestyle and previous way of thinking and had this to say:

"When I made a decision that I was going to live pure until marriage, it was after I had already had sex with over a hundred women. Just imagine all those connectivities to all those women. So when I made a decision after I learned what this was doing to those women and what it was doing to me, I made a decision that I was going to wait until marriage, and I had to really allow the Holy Spirit to cleanse me of all those soul ties. Those are very difficult to break.

And these women didn't understand it from the biblical perspective: I had sex with you, and you are another man's wife technically. I had to really try to cleanse myself from all of those things and allow God to do a great work inside of me. Unfortunately, that's not something that was prevented because I didn't get any training on how I should've been operating beforehand. I think that if I had waited, I would've been able to make sure and hold this special gift that God gave me and give it to my wife and say nobody has ever had what you're having, and that wasn't something I could do.

If you don't wait and you don't have the proper relationship that is biblical—where you're connected to the person and understand them as a friend, and it's just all physical—the problem is you're going not to want anything to do with that person after you physically had sex with them. You're not going to have any spiritual or emotional connection to them. You may have a physical connection to them while it feels good, but when the pleasure stops, there's no substance. The Bible teaches the way where there is substance to relationships when you do it God's way versus when you don't. If I could change it, I would do it all over again, do it differently, and wait. I think there's value in that. I don't care if they call you square or whatever. Nobody can tell you what that treasure is worth except you and God."

Psychologically, individuals may experience confusion and emotional instability. In a non-committed context, sexual encounters often lack the emotional security and trust found in committed relationships, leading to feelings of emptiness, anxiety, and even depression. The separation of sex from emotional intimacy can cause individuals to struggle with attachment, resulting in lower self-esteem and an increased sense of vulnerability. Research shows that casual sexual encounters often correlate with regret, dissatisfaction, and reduced mental well-being, especially when expectations of emotional connection go unmet.

Societally, the detachment of sex from commitment can weaken social structures, particularly those related to family and community. Historically, sex within marriage helped to form strong family units, creating a stable environment for raising children and fostering a sense of communal responsibility. In cultures that prioritize casual sex, the erosion of these structures can lead to the breakdown of families, increased divorce rates, and an unstable environment for children, all of which negatively impact society's collective mental and emotional health. In sum, when sex is removed from a commitment-centered framework, it not only impacts individuals' mental health but also weakens broader social bonds, contributing to a culture that is less stable and more prone to emotional harm and exploitation.

One of the proven contributors to exploitation and sexual abuse is early sexualization. With the plethora of negative consequences that come from premarital sex, some additional dangers and harms come with sexual exposure at an early age. When individuals are exposed to or engage in sexual activity at an early age, they often have not fully developed the emotional maturity needed to navigate sexual relationships. This can make it difficult for them to set clear boundaries, making them more vulnerable to manipulation. Predators often exploit this lack of boundary-setting, pressuring or coercing young individuals into situations they aren't prepared for.

20 years ago, with less access to digital devices and internet access, children also had less access to pornography and sexually explicit material. And with each year, and rapid technological advances, today's youth are being exposed to more and more. I recently saw a statement saying that today's youth have seen more sexual and violent material than previous generations had in their entire adult lives. Let that sink in for a moment. And because younger and younger children are being exposed to glamorized casual, non-committed sex, they are hardly able to discern healthy relationships, signs of coercion or manipulation, and have a significantly greater risk of being susceptible to abuse themselves.

The early sexualization of individuals has profound conse-quences, especially as younger people are often more vulnerable to manipulation and exploitation, leading to cycles of abuse that can persist into adulthood. Studies have consistently linked casual sex to elevated rates of anxiety and depression, particularly when it occurs without emotional support or commitment. The fleeting pleasure of such encounters can often give way to feelings of emptiness or loneliness if deeper emotional needs remain unmet, contributing over time to cycles of low self-worth and emotional instability, which can lead to broader mental health challenges.

Beyond pornographic content, media and mainstream culture increasingly normalize aggressive and non-consensual sexual behavior, shaping perceptions of relationships in ways that can be harmful. For instance, much of the content in mainstream pornography includes depictions of coercive or violent sex, reinforcing the notion that these dynamics are acceptable. This exposure not only desensitizes viewers to boundaries but can lead them to tolerate or even engage in similar behaviors within their relationships. Furthermore, pornography frequently objectifies individuals, particularly women, reducing them to their sexual roles and erasing their agency. This kind of dehumanization can seep into casual encounters, fostering a mindset in which partners are valued solely for physical gratification rather than as whole individuals with emotional and psychological needs.

One of the most dangerous aspects of popular pornography is the perversion of regular scenarios and daily activities. Common examples include things like "teacher has sex with student," "husband cheats on wife with housemaid," or "employee earns bonus from boss at work." Perverted scenarios like these infiltrate the minds of men, causing them to obscure actual life events and situations. Psychologists even believe that the increasing sexual violence towards housemaids, students, and work employees is directly tied to pornography's portrayal of these events. Released court records reveal an increasing number of men who argue that the women accusing them of sexual crimes were "giving them signs of consent." These records go on to describe "signs of consent" being eye contact, early arrival, or being foreign and having a language barrier—all signs commonly associated with consent in pornographic storylines. This is just an example of how pornographic addictions and interests can fuel sexual violence and exploitation.

When I reflect on my time at Howard University, I remember conversations with men and women who were in complicated sexual relationships that bordered on abuse and exploitation. I remember hearing my female friends talk about encounters with boyfriends where they were drinking together and felt like they had been taken advantage of. I also remember conversations with my male friends who were navigating the complexities of finding out that sex they believed was consensual had been perceived as coerced by women they were dating. This was my exposure to how commonly these lines get blurred when there is no commitment or covenant. In my reflection, the only ones of us who had 100% protection against being convicted or accused of any sexual crimes were those of us who were committed to purity. Our decisions to remain abstinent automatically deterred these issues and headaches.

In the past, I compromised my abstinence by telling lies about my life. I was avoiding all sexual relationships while giving in to society's pressures. I knew men wouldn't think I was cool if they knew I was abstinent, so I practiced a life of purity in secret. And to make matters worse, to fit in, I often would lie and say I was having sex even though I wasn't. In the worst cases, I tainted the reputations of other women by lying about having sexual encounters with them. This continued until one day, the LORD convicted me about how my lies were, in fact, equal to me doing the very acts I was abstaining from. If I was going to hide my purity and therefore rob God of receiving glory from my decision, then I might as well have been having sex like the other men who hadn't committed to purity. And in obedience to the LORD, I did the difficult work of confessing the truth to all the men I had lied to. I'll never forget how embarrassing it felt to tell them, "Hey. Remember when I told you I had sex with Monica? The truth is that I lied."

Because pleasing God was most important to me, I no longer cared about my reputation or what the other men would think of me. I wanted to be free from needing man's approval and to allow my decision to remain abstinent to inspire others to live for God. And to my surprise, the LORD rewarded my obedience by having all those men respond graciously to my confession. It inspired many of them to be honest with me about things they had also lied about, teaching me that many men avoid the truth to gain approval from others. If men can push past the cultural pressures and recognize the bigger picture, we can truly impact the world.

The Bible, while often misquoted and misunderstood, presents a very high view of marriage, sexual integrity, and sexual conduct. Even some of the laws in the Old Testament that we would consider outdated or obsolete reveal God's heart for a society that valued marriage and prioritized healthy sexual relations within the confines of marriage. Chapters like Leviticus 18 or even specific passages like Leviticus 20:10 define appropriate sexual relationships and present the death penalty as punishment for adultery. Deuteronomy 22:13-29, for example, discusses various scenarios of sexual misconduct, including adultery, premarital sex, and rape. It covers the responsibilities of men and the protection of women's rights, such as the punishment for a man who rapes a virgin and the command to marry her if she was not betrothed. While these laws reflect ancient Israel's cultural and religious context, they emphasize the importance of maintaining family structures, sexual purity, and respect between men and women. They also make the clear connection that what we do with our physical bodies affects and correlates to our spiritual connection and relationship with a Holy God. We'll talk more about the spiritual dynamics of sex in chapter 6, but we need to understand that the entire Bible promotes sex being reserved for the marriage covenant.

I specifically chose to highlight Old Testament passages here because, generally, most people are familiar with the New Testament's stance on marriage. Instead, they usually fail to see the cohesion within both testaments and how God's high view of the marriage covenant deters violence and abuse in society. For readers unaware of the popular New Testament scriptures that support marital sexual relations, see 1 Corinthians 6:12-20 or any

 Why men shouldn't have sex before marriage

of the other places where Paul writes about the importance of honoring God with our bodies.

Contrary to popular opinion, what the Bible teaches explicitly about male leadership is hardly ever divorced from covenantal relationships. This radically goes against what mainstream society tries to depict as the Bible's patriarchal stance on the order of society. In reality, the Bible speaks about men being the leaders of their wives and their homes—not saying that men in and of themselves are the leaders of all of society. This is an important distinction, as without it, much abuse and patriarchal misunderstanding has occurred. Using this framework serves as the primary support for my call for greater leadership amongst men—beginning with the men who are reading this book. Although not expressly written as a promotion of marriage, this book is tied heavily to marriage because the marriage covenant provides the clearest framework for male leadership. It defines who men are leading, creating healthy parameters for their leadership.

Men who are married and have families hardly have questions about who they are in charge of and who they are responsible for. While this may seem like a call for every man to get married, it is more so a call to understand that your leadership is connected to those with whom you've built trust, love, and respect. Because covenant relationships can also include platonic friendships, men can be leaders in every relationship where they have committed to be sacrificial, loving, respectful, and caring. As it relates to what we've been speaking about regarding premarital sex, it further shows that men who lead the charge in their covenantal relationships by intentionally being leaders in the area of purity create ripple effects that touch every area of society. We are often inundated with the historical societies of the ancient Romans and Greeks that were known for going awry due to the rampant abuse of male and patriarchal leadership. However, the biblical call for manhood and male leadership is entirely different. And if the men reading this book understand that, there will be a more excellent opportunity for this world to lean into the dynamic that the Lord has designed for us because the leading men are gentle, sacrificial leaders rather than power-hungry, double-standard leaders.

The call to be men who preserve sex solely for the covenant of marriage begins with the decision in our heart that is firmly rooted in a love for God and a love for neighbor. We will discuss this in the next chapter as we cover abstinence's long-term impact on marriage and marital happiness.

CHAPTER 4:

Laying the Groundwork: Marriage and Long-Term Happiness

Many people have fallen into the trap of believing that what they do before marriage stays in the past and has no bearing on their future. This dangerous lie has led many to think they can indulge in multiple sexual relationships and then, with the flip of a switch, suddenly become a one-woman man once they decide to settle down. It's almost like trying to win a championship game without ever practicing or preparing for it. Marriage, after all, is the ultimate commitment. It's a lifelong promise to remain emotionally, physically, and spiritually faithful to one person. Why, then, would anyone think that not preparing for that level of commitment beforehand would lead to success?

It seems absurd to believe that engaging in sexual relationships with multiple partners would somehow help us focus entirely on one person for the rest of our lives. Science tells us that sex isn't just a physical act—it's deeply emotional and chemical as well. Sex releases hormones, like oxytocin and vasopressin, which are meant to bond us to our partner on an emotional level. So why do we ignore the reality that forming these bonds with numerous people before marriage could weaken our ability to wholly and exclusively bond with one spouse for a lifetime? Can we really give ourselves 100% to our spouse after sharing those bonds with others? It raises a critical question about the emotional consequences of premarital sex: how does it affect our ability to maintain fidelity and emotional intimacy in marriage?

We'll also look at some hard numbers. What do the divorce statistics say about couples who waited until marriage versus those who didn't? Are couples who were virgins before marriage more satisfied in their relationships than those who had previous partners? You might be surprised at what the research reveals.

This chapter will dive deeply into how premarital sex has long-lasting effects on both marriage and marital happiness. We'll examine real-life examples of men who waited until marriage to have sex and hear how their decision has positively impacted their marriages. Through their stories, we'll see the long-term benefits of abstinence and how it lays a stronger foundation for a lasting, healthy marriage. Alongside personal testimonies, we will explore the spiritual and emotional dimensions that come into play when we choose to engage in premarital sex. Finally, we will examine the scientific evidence confirming how these decisions impact us well into our married lives. By the end of this chapter, it will be apparent that our choices before marriage don't just stay in the past—they follow us into our future.

One of the most profound revelations I've come to in recent years is this: man was made for God. We live in a world that constantly tries to tell us our purpose, and the "purpose discovery" industry has become one of the most lucrative fields today. Many religious leaders, theologians, and clergy have sought to answer the question: "What is my purpose?" This question is asked so frequently because people, whether religious or not, deeply desire to know why they were created and what they are meant to do. If marketed well, anyone claiming to have the answer could easily become wealthy. Motivational speakers, spiritual guides, and life coaches have built entire careers writing books and designing programs to help others tap into their potential and discover their purpose. But the truth is that offering people any purpose less than their true one merely satisfies a temporary need, leaving them continually searching for more.

So, what is our real purpose? The Bible paints a compelling picture of a God who owned everything yet still felt incomplete without human creation. In Genesis, we read that humans were made in God's image and likeness. Theologically, this means we are the only creation capable of both interacting with and comprehending our Creator. We are the ones who can hear His voice and engage in meaningful relationship with Him. Once we understand that God created man for His purpose, pleasure, and glory, it changes how we view everything else in life. It becomes clear that a man who is made for God must seek to live in a way that is pleasing to Him. This means we must actively seek to know God's heart so we can live a life aligned with His commands and decrees. Fulfilling our purpose is intrinsically tied to our obedience to God.

When it comes to the conversation about sex, the same principle applies. If God has given us a command regarding sex, any disobedience to that command is not just a moral misstep—it is a deviation from our true purpose. This leads to an important question: beyond pleasing God, does following His commands actually benefit us, His creation? The Bible provides a clear answer. Throughout scripture, we see that God's will for His people is to prosper. In Deuteronomy 29:9, Moses tells the Israelites that the Lord gave them commands and words of the covenant "so that He may prosper them." Similarly, in John 10:10, Jesus declares, "I came that they may have life and have it abundantly." In Jeremiah 29:11, we are reminded: "For I know the plans I have for you, declares the Lord, plans for welfare and not for evil, to give you a future and a hope."

These scriptures reveal that God's commands are not arbitrary restrictions but the pathway to human flourishing. A man who is obedient to God has the best chance of living the abundant, full life for which he was created. This leads to a somewhat circular but profound conclusion. If we were created for God, and obedience to Him brings us closer to our purpose, then disobedience distances us from that purpose. In this context, violating God's command to reserve sex for the covenant of marriage doesn't just affect our behavior—it hinders our ability to know the God who created us for a relationship with Himself. Disobedience hardens our hearts and blinds our eyes to God's presence, distancing us spiritually. This is part of the spiritual consequence of premarital sex. Engaging in sex outside of marriage leads to spiritual death, creating dissonance between us and God.

One of my favorite aspects of the Bible is its teaching that we become like what we worship. In the story of ancient Israel, we see the people either becoming more alive as they worshiped the living God or more dead as they worshiped lifeless idols. The reason I bring this up is that premarital sex has spiritual consequences that mirror this biblical principle. Research supports the idea that a solid spiritual foundation is the strongest predictor of marital success. Even non-religious psychologists and sociologists are beginning to recognize that sex is not merely a physical act—it's a spiritual one, carrying with it the potential for both blessings and curses. Those who engage in sex outside of marriage often struggle to find spiritual direction and stability, while those who choose abstinence experience blessings and deeper connections both to each other and to the God who designed marriage.

In addition to the chemical bonding that occurs through sex, it also has a profound impact on an individual's spiritual life, often reshaping beliefs and priorities. As a minister, I've seen many people make solid commitments to walk faithfully with God, dedicating themselves to living for Him. These individuals typically maintained strong spiritual lives for extended periods, yet one of the most consistent reasons for them eventually drifting away from their faith was linked to their sexual decisions. I began to notice a recurring pattern: when people entered romantic and sexual relationships, it often resulted in a significant pull away from their spiritual foundation.

I've mentored numerous young men who were confident that their new relationship with Jesus was unshakable. Yet, once they began engaging in a sexual relationship with someone they deeply cared about, their spiritual life often faltered. This is because premarital sex disrupts a person's spiritual grounding. It gradually becomes a dominant part of life, overshadowing their commitment to spiritual growth and purity. While sexual attraction and intimacy are healthy and vital within the context of marriage, outside of marriage, sex often leads to spiritual disconnection.

Sex's natural magnetic pull is designed to draw couples together, helping them remain emotionally and physically connected as they journey through life. But for men committed to a life of purity and obedience to God, opening the door to premarital sex frequently marks the beginning of spiritual decline. As scripture reminds us, "God is a jealous God" and only allows room for those committed to following His ways. The reality is that sexual sin doesn't just affect one's relationship with a partner—it pulls them away from their spiritual life and their community, ultimately distancing them from the God they once followed so passionately.

Here's a story illustrating how premarital sex wars against our individual and united spiritual growth:

Noah and Maria met during their college years, and both were drawn to each other quickly and intensely. It wasn't long before they began a sexual relationship, wrapped up in the excitement of being together. Although neither of them had been deeply religious, something stirred in Noah a few years later when a friend invited him to church. Curious and feeling an emptiness in his life that he couldn't quite explain, he decided to attend. Surprised by how much the message resonated with him, he started going regularly. Soon, he asked Maria to join him, thinking this could be the answer to some of the restlessness they had both felt in their relationship.

Maria was hesitant initially, but like Noah, she sensed a void that needed filling. The more they attended church together, the more involved they became. The congregation was welcoming, and the couple found inspiration in the other members, particularly the married couples who seemed spiritually and emotionally connected. Their example sparked hope for Noah and Maria, who began to believe that church was the key to addressing the deep spiritual longing they had never fully acknowledged.

They committed to growing spiritually as they began taking their faith more seriously. However, there was one area where they struggled: they couldn't completely stop having sex with each other. They would go weeks, sometimes months, without falling back into old habits, but each time they did, guilt followed. At first, they would confess to people they trusted, hold themselves accountable, and promise to do better. But over time, the weight of their failure began to grow heavier. They were fully aware of their decisions' impact on their spiritual growth, yet they felt powerless to stop. The more they slipped, the more ashamed they felt, especially as they saw other couples thriving in their faith.

Noah and Maria had sought help from their pastor once before, confessing their struggle and looking for guidance. The church's advice was difficult but straightforward: it was suggested that they take a break from each other, focus on strengthening their individual relationships with God, and avoid situations where temptation could easily overtake them. But they brushed off this counsel, believing they could figure it out on their own. They convinced themselves that their spiritual growth could coexist with their physical desires. Boundaries weren't set, and the allure of sex continued to sabotage their efforts.

Months went by, and the cycle continued. Eventually, the couple grew frustrated and disillusioned. Unable to reconcile their spiritual aspirations with their physical actions, they concluded that church wasn't for them. They left the congregation, believing that they could maintain their connection to each other without the spiritual accountability they once sought. Soon after, they eloped, convinced their love alone was strong enough to weather whatever storms came their way.

At first, marriage felt like a fresh start. But it wasn't long before the cracks began to show. The spiritual unity they had once aimed for was never fully realized, and soon they found themselves drifting in opposite directions. Still holding onto the conviction that they should be active in a faith community, Noah was never fully at peace with their absence from church. He longed for the deep spiritual connection that had once felt so promising. Maria, on the other hand, had no interest in returning. The pressure they had experienced trying to reconcile their faith with their physical relationship had left her feeling traumatized, and she vowed never to put herself in that situation again.

As the months passed, their intimacy began to falter. Sex, once the center of their connection, no longer felt satisfying. They couldn't understand why, but their physical relationship seemed to have lost its spark. What they didn't realize was that their intimacy was suffering because it had never been rooted in a deeper, spiritual foundation. The connection they longed for couldn't be sustained through physical acts alone. Without a shared spiritual grounding, their physical and emotional intimacy was destined to fall short.

Noah continued to wrestle with his faith, torn between his desire for spiritual growth and his love for Maria, who had shut herself off from any possibility of returning to church. They had built a relationship without a firm foundation of spiritual unity, and now, as a married couple, they were paying the price. The bond they once felt so sure of was unraveling, and without a shared spiritual vision, they were left with little to hold them together.

This story illustrates the importance of building a solid spiritual foundation before marriage. Noah and Maria's struggles highlight how crucial it is for couples to establish spiritual unity without relying on physical intimacy to hold their relationship together. By rejecting the guidance they were given and neglecting to set firm boundaries, they failed to grow together spiritually. Their experience serves as a cautionary tale for those who believe they can thrive without first building a united spiritual foundation—because, in the long run, without it, both their relationship and their intimacy are bound to suffer.

Research shows that a shared spiritual foundation is the strongest foundation for a successful marriage. When couples engage in premarital sex, they not only jeopardize a crucial aspect of this spiritual foundation but may also limit how much they can grow spiritually together in the future. Marriage is inherently challenging, and every marriage requires hard work, commitment, and resilience to thrive. Given these demands, couples must build a solid spiritual base during their dating phase, as the spiritual practices they establish will become the "muscles" they rely on throughout their married life.

Surveys of Christian couples suggest that those who engaged in premarital sex often struggled with guilt and shame, which became barriers to engaging in shared spiritual activities like praying, reading scripture, or attending religious services. This disconnect hindered their ability to create the strong spiritual foundation needed for the challenges of marriage. On the other hand, couples who committed to abstinence reported higher levels of spiritual intentionality, better communication, improved conflict resolution, and a stronger connection to spiritual practices such as prayer, Bible study, and community involvement. These spiritual practices during dating strengthened their future marriage and helped them align in important areas like career, family planning, and community service.

Furthermore, couples who prioritized abstinence were often more focused on social justice and community engagement, qualities that contribute to the health and longevity of a marriage. These shared values and goals—grounded in a united spiritual foundation—help marriages thrive over the long term. In essence, building a marriage on spiritual unity is crucial for navigating the inevitable challenges, empowering couples to face them together and ensuring a lasting, fulfilling relationship.

One scripture often misquoted and taken out of context is 2 Corinthians 6:14: *"Do not be unequally yoked with unbelievers. For what partnership has righteousness with lawlessness? Or what fellowship has light with darkness?"* To properly understand and interpret this verse, we must first consider the context and the culture from which it originates. With this in mind, we should ask: What does it mean to be "yoked"?

A yoke is a wooden device that binds two animals together to work in tandem. Once yoked, they are locked into a partnership that neither can escape without outside intervention. Therefore, when Paul uses the term "yoked" in this verse, he is describing a deep bond—one that, in this case, mirrors a covenant relationship. He is not referring merely to friendships with unbelievers, as Jesus himself maintained relationships with non-believers, such as tax collectors and sinners. The criticism Jesus received for such associations shows us that relationships with unbelievers are not prohibited but must be understood within a proper context.

Paul further clarifies this idea by referencing God's Old Testament command for Israel to "go out from their midst" and "be separate from them." This command warned Israel not to intermarry with other nations that worshipped false gods. The concern was that such unions would lead to spiritual compromise, tempting Israel to adopt idolatrous practices. Therefore, this text is not about casual relationships but rather about entering into a covenant, such as marriage, with someone who does not share the same faith.

For Christians, this becomes a clear mandate: we are not to enter into marriage with someone who does not share our faith in Jesus Christ. The reason for this is evident. Here's a quote from Tim Keller in his book "The Meaning of Marriage" about this. Tim says, "The essence of intimacy in marriage is that finally you have someone who will eventually come to understand you and accept you as you are. Your spouse should be someone you don't have to hide from or always be "spinning"; it should be

 Why men shouldn't have sex before marriage

someone who "gets" you. But if the person is not a believer, he or she can't understand your very essence and heart. If you do marry someone who does not share your faith, then there are only two ways to proceed. One is that you will more and more have to lose your transparency. In the normal, healthy Christian life, you relate Christ and the gospel to everything. You will think of Christ when watching a movie. You will base decisions on Christian principles. You will think about what you read in the Bible that day. But if you are natural and transparent about all of these thoughts, your partner will find it at least tedious or annoying and even offensive. He or she will say, "I had no idea you were this overboard about your faith." You will just have to hide it all. The other, worse possibility is that you move Christ out of a central place in your consciousness. You will have to let your heart's ardor for Christ cool. You will have to deliberately not think out how your Christian commitment relates to every area of your life. You will demote Christ in your mind and heart, because if you keep him central, you will feel isolated from your spouse. Both of these possible outcomes are, of course, terrible. That is why you should not deliberately marry someone who does not share your Christian faith."

Keller emphasizes that being unequally yoked in marriage leads to a lifetime of spiritual compromise. One spouse will always be pulled in the direction of abandoning their faith to maintain harmony in the marriage, or they will face the constant tension of trying to follow Christ while their partner moves in the opposite direction.

God wants us to avoid this difficult and unnecessary struggle. That's why He instructs us to marry those who share the same spiritual goals and commitment. An equally yoked couple can walk together in unity, support one another, and share the burden of life's challenges as they pursue the same purpose.

This kind of unity, however, must be intentionally cultivated and does not happen by chance. Furthermore, it is significantly hindered in relationships where premarital sex is present, as physical intimacy can cloud judgment and make it more difficult to build the spiritual foundation that marriage requires.

In the late 1990s and early 2000s, there was a push amongst high school education programs to begin incorporating early marriage education classes designed to help correct the rampant and growing divorce problem that was starting to affect many marriages in the country. While each state that decided to implement this program had drastically different views and opinions about the curriculum and what it would include, one of the biggest discrepancies between the programs was whether they merely focused on communication and dating habits or whether they also included abstinence and sexual education. This was in response to the consistent statistics showing that couples that engage in premarital sex before marriage often have a higher divorce rate and report less satisfaction in their marriages. The Institute on Religion and Public Life published an article by Dana Mack in 2001 saying this: "In pretending that there is no connection between current dating behaviors and young people's ultimate goal of happy, permanent unions, many high school marriage programs do nothing to discourage the kind of casual sex that hardens young people and foments distrust between men and women. But worse, in addressing the challenges of sexually intimate relationships as generic communication problems, these programs may lead young people into believing that communication "skills" are all that it takes to make marriages work."

Studies have shown that couples who wait to have sex until marriage often have lower divorce rates. A study from the Institute for Family Studies indicates that those who waited to have sex until after marriage had a 22% lower chance of divorce compared to those who engaged in premarital sex. This may be because waiting helps couples enter marriage with clearer intentions and a better understanding of commitment.

Current dating culture promotes the idea that sexual experience with multiple people is necessary before getting married. This belief is so widespread that now, 50% of people in the US have more than five sexual partners before they get married. However, according to scientific studies and a new study by the Wheatley Institute, statistics show that having multiple sexual partners before marriage decreases marriage quality in four significant ways. The first way is relationship satisfaction, which indicates that abstinent individuals are 2x more likely to be very satisfied in their marriages. The second way was relationship stability, showing that spouses who had only had sex with their spouse were 3x more likely to have stable marriages.

The third way is the area of sexual satisfaction. Couples who remain abstinent until marriage are 2x more likely to be satisfied with their marital sex lives. Only 1 in 14 people who were sexually active before marriage reported that they were sexually satisfied in their marriage. And the final category that was assessed by the Wheatley Institute's study was emotional connection. Research revealed that nearly 80% of sexually inexperienced couples reported the highest level of emotional connection within their marriage, which is 20% higher than individuals who have had multiple sexual partners before marriage. These findings challenge the notion that sexual experience helps individuals have healthier marriages and prove the exact opposite. The truth remains that sexual exclusivity fuels intimacy and fortifies the relationship for the difficulties of marriage.

Building on our earlier explanation about how premarital sex does not align with the preparation for a long-term, monogamous marriage, it's also crucial to recognize how abstinence cultivates self-discipline and respect for your future spouse in several key ways.

First, abstinence fosters self-control and resilience. A man who has practiced delaying gratification will be better prepared for marriage, where the need for patience and self-control is ongoing. Learning to resist temptation and manage desire equips a man to handle times when his spouse may not share the same mood or sex drive. This preparation helps him navigate seasons when sex may need to wait, such as when dealing with work, children, or other responsibilities. For men who never practiced this discipline, marriage can be a shock as they face the realities of life where sex isn't always immediately available. Abstinence helps create emotional stability in men, preparing them to be patient and avoid anger or frustration when intimacy is delayed.

This skill becomes particularly important during times such as pregnancy or postpartum, where sex might not be possible for extended periods. Maintaining emotional, spiritual, and mental unity is vital during such times to ensure a healthy relationship. Drawing from our earlier metaphor comparing a relationship to a house, physical intimacy is like the decoration—it enhances comfort but isn't foundational. Studies show that infidelity often peaks during pregnancy and postpartum when physical bonding is less frequent. This underscores the need for men to understand that marriage is not all about sex and to develop habits of delaying gratification in preparation for marriage.

Abstinence, in this sense, strengthens character and establishes moral and ethical boundaries, which are necessary to handle temptations that continue even after marriage. This is especially true for men, who, as visual creatures, benefit from abstinence by developing the strength to navigate temptations with integrity and faithfulness.

Second, abstinence fosters mutual respect between partners. Choosing to remain abstinent is a way of demonstrating deep appreciation and respect for one's future spouse. Men who wait until marriage understand the sacredness of sex and its emotional and spiritual significance. By saving this act for their spouse, they communicate that their partner is worth the wait. This attitude isn't just about sexual purity but extends to honoring their spouse's body, emotions, and future together.

For many, the wedding night becomes a profoundly sacred moment where they can fully give themselves to one another, knowing they have held back until now. Abstinence communicates a hopeful view of the future. By living for the future rather than immediate gratification, men show their spouses that they've always anticipated a special and meaningful union. This sense of value and security can strengthen marriage in ways that are often absent among couples who do not wait.

Abstinence signals that both individuals value their relationship's emotional and spiritual aspects over temporary physical satisfaction, which fosters a deeper connection in the long run.

Third, abstinence helps set the stage for a lasting and satisfying marriage. Couples prioritizing abstinence tend to have a more long-term vision for their relationship. Because their dating relationship wasn't built on momentary physical pleasure, they focused on shared values, personal goals, and faith, which helped establish a foundation for long-term success.

These relationships are often more resilient, as couples invest deeply in each other's futures, supporting each other's ambitions. Such relationships are grounded less on superficial aspects and more on enduring values that will continue to nourish the marriage.

Finally, abstinence before marriage offers couples the chance to begin with a clean slate. Entering into marriage without the emotional and physical baggage of past sexual experiences reduces the likelihood of comparisons to previous partners. It promotes sexual and emotional exclusivity, contributing to a more fulfilling and satisfying marital relationship. Couples who have abstained start their marriage with a fresh perspective, unburdened by the complexities of previous relationships, setting them up for a healthier and more rewarding journey together.

In essence, abstinence cultivates the qualities of self-discipline, respect, and commitment that are essential for a successful marriage, laying the groundwork for a relationship built on emotional, spiritual, and physical fulfillment.

Of the men I interviewed who were virgins until marriage, all rated their marital satisfaction at least 8 out of 10. Moreover, they all gave their sexual satisfaction a perfect 10 out of 10. A common reason for this high sexual satisfaction was that they had no basis for comparison, meaning that their only experience was also their best experience. This perspective seemed to contribute positively to their outlook on both marriage and sex.

In addition to these high satisfaction ratings, all of these men expressed no regrets about waiting until marriage to have sex. They firmly believed that this decision had enriched their sexual relationship and overall marriage. Looking back, they felt their marriages were stronger because of their choice to remain abstinent. However, like men who didn't wait until marriage, they still found their actual experiences of sex and marriage to be different from their expectations. The main distinction was that virgin men entered marriage with a more humble view of sex, seeing it as something to grow and learn within their relationship. In contrast, men with previous sexual experience often assumed their marital sex life would naturally meet or exceed prior experiences, leading to comparisons and overlooking the emotional aspects of sex.

Despite their humility, virgin men often shared a common misconception with non-virgin men: both expected that sex would be a daily occurrence in marriage. Many were surprised to find this wasn't the case. However, virgin men reported having more frequent sexual encounters than men who had been sexually active before marriage. Virgin men who married virgin women had the highest levels of satisfaction and reported having sex five out of seven days a week. These encounters were both planned and spontaneous and were free from pressure to maintain specific levels of intensity or duration. The data indicates that virgin couples enjoy sex most frequently, with less pressure to meet specific performance standards.

When two people commit to abstinence before marriage, they make a powerful statement about their priorities and values. This mutual decision to wait creates a foundation of trust and respect, as each partner demonstrates their willingness to put the relationship's long-term well-being above immediate gratification. This trust often carries over into marriage, as both individuals have already proven their capacity for patience, self-discipline, and commitment.

Couples who practice abstinence often report feeling more respected by their partners. This is because the act of waiting until marriage for sexual intimacy symbolizes a deep respect for the emotional, physical, and spiritual connection they hope to share. Knowing that each person values the union enough to wait can foster a sense of worth and significance, which deepens their emotional bond.

For many, abstinence is not just a personal or relational decision but a spiritual one. Abstinence can align one's actions with spiritual beliefs, which can bring a greater sense of purpose and meaning to the relationship. Couples who view sex as something sacred are likely to see their marriage as a spiritual partnership. Abstaining from sex before marriage can strengthen this bond, as both individuals share a common goal of honoring their spiritual convictions.

In a marriage built on these shared values, couples often find that their spiritual connection becomes a source of strength during challenging times. Abstinence before marriage can create a sense of shared purpose, allowing each partner to feel supported not only by their spouse but also by a shared belief system. This shared spiritual connection can act as a guiding force in the marriage, providing a sense of security, fostering resilience, unity, and a shared vision for the future.

By choosing to abstain, couples also experience an enhanced sense of excitement and anticipation as they approach marriage. Because they have not yet experienced sexual intimacy, the wedding night and subsequent honeymoon can carry a sense of newness and discovery. For some, this "waiting" period heightens the significance of sexual intimacy, making it a profound and memorable part of the marriage journey.

The choice to wait often leads to a deeper appreciation of sex as an act of love and connection rather than merely a physical experience. For couples who value this perspective, the decision to abstain can foster an intimate bond that goes beyond the physical, as they perceive their sexual relationship as an expression of their emotional and spiritual commitment to one another.

Entering into marriage without previous sexual relationships or experiences allows many couples to start with a "clean slate." This lack of prior sexual history can minimize comparisons to past partners, reducing insecurities and enhancing a sense of exclusivity. It's not uncommon for those who abstain to feel that they have a unique connection with their spouse that no one else shares. This exclusivity often helps couples to feel bonded on a deeper level and contributes to a strong foundation of trust.

Additionally, when there is no residual baggage from past sexual relationships, couples are less likely to carry unresolved emotional issues into their marriage. This sense of a fresh start enhances the emotional and spiritual closeness between partners, as they can build a new life together without outside influences affecting their bond.

Virgin men are not immune to temptation and reported experiencing it as frequently as men who were not virgins. However, the nature and impact of temptation differed significantly between these two groups. While virgins experienced attraction and temptation similarly, they exhibited much less curiosity about exploring sex outside their marriage. For men who had multiple past partners, temptation often involved memories of previous sexual experiences triggered by physical similarities with other women. This lingering association can create a mental hurdle, especially for men who may feel less satisfied in their marriages.

If a study were conducted comparing rates of infidelity between men who were virgins before marriage and those who were not, it would likely show higher infidelity rates among men with prior sexual experience. This is due to their relatively lower levels of marital and sexual satisfaction, which can exacerbate feelings of temptation. For virgin men, while temptation may arise, the curiosity to seek new sexual experiences is generally absent. This difference highlights the value of abstinence before marriage: it fosters discipline that carries over into married life, equipping men to resist temptation with the same self-control practiced before marriage.

This concept is especially relevant for men in leadership, such as pastors or public figures, who face significant challenges related to sexual temptation and moral failure. Many of these men, though professing deliverance from sexual addictions, may not fully recognize the lasting damage that their previous lifestyle has inflicted. For men in these roles—and for all men—it's vital to stay close to their wives, nurturing their marriage as a safeguard against temptation. Ultimately, this is not just about sexual discipline but about the possibility of spiritual renewal. Any man can reclaim his integrity, regardless of past choices, by committing to change today.

One of the profound truths embedded in Genesis 3, where Adam and Eve disobey God in the Garden, is that their sin and disobedience hurt them in ways God never intended. They believed the serpent's lie that God was withholding something good from them, which led them to take what God had forbidden. Notably, the Bible doesn't suggest that the fruit itself was inherently bad; rather, it was the act of disobedience that was damaging. This distinction is important: God's prohibitions don't necessarily mean that what is off-limits is bad but that disobeying His instructions leads to harm.

In the same way, God's command to abstain from premarital sex isn't because sex itself is bad but because going against this guidance hurts us in ways God doesn't want. After Adam and Eve's disobedience, they immediately experienced disunity, illustrated by Adam blaming Eve when God held him accountable. This was the first recorded instance of disunity between them, emphasizing a broader spiritual truth: disobedience to God's commands creates division between people who were meant to be united.

This principle is observable when comparing premarital sex to waiting until marriage. Those who engage in premarital sex often experience disunity in their relationships, including in marriage, because premarital sex fosters patterns of self-centeredness, mistrust, and comparison. God wants men and women to be united and for spouses to trust each other implicitly, feeling like true allies, not adversaries.

Psychologist John Gottman, who has extensively studied relationships, identifies contempt and a lack of compassion as major predictors of divorce. This is similar to the disunity Adam showed toward Eve when he shifted blame to her, portraying her as a barrier to his obedience to God. From my interviews, it was apparent that virgin men often view their wives as partners who help them fulfill their potential. Had I asked, "How much do you believe your wife helps you reach your maximum potential?" instead of asking for a satisfaction rating, I am confident the answers would align with the ratings. Premarital sex, unless healed by God, distorts perceptions and breeds division in relationships.

Relationships have a unique power: they are both where we are most deeply hurt and where we can be most profoundly healed. For those desiring strong, lasting marriages, it is beneficial to follow God's commands and recognize that it isn't the activity itself that's bad—sex, in this case—but rather engaging in it outside of God's design. Sex is good within marriage, but sex outside of marriage is where the harm lies.

When I had sex with my girlfriend at 16 years old, I didn't know that I was gambling with my life. I didn't know that many men in my position—who loved God, knew that sex should only be reserved for marriage, and had parents teach them about the dangers of having sex before its time—had also strayed away from what they knew was right. But I wasn't mindful that many of those men never returned. I was naive to the addictive nature of sex, and it is by God's grace that my one sexual encounter was my only and last encounter until marriage. It was my first serious relationship, and I was dating a girl at my high school who was raised very differently. Looking back, I realized how long I've had a savior complex, as I considered her my newest evangelism project. I was aware that she hadn't grown up in a church home and that divorced parents had raised her. I loved and was attracted to the idea that she was somewhat wild and untamed. From her perspective, she was so unfamiliar with Christianity and the idea that there were men who loved Jesus, believed in the Bible, and wanted to do what God said. Because of this, she found me interesting and attractive. It was the unknown curiosity of each other's lives that drew us close to each other.

I was her introduction to the church, the first person she read the Bible with, and she loved being around my family and experiencing the warmth of my home. At that age, I wasn't disturbed by her many past partners; instead, I was even drawn to the idea of having a "freaky" girlfriend who was openly sexual. Somehow, I convinced myself that I was strong enough to handle who she was with the strength of who I was. For much of our relationship, I had a stronger influence. Her friends took pride in her spiritual and emotional changes, which seemed to reflect a real transformation within her. But while she was growing, I was weakening in my resolve to stay abstinent until marriage. My church upbringing had taught me that purity was an expression of our love for God, not just a distant mandate. However, as time passed, her constant pressure to have sex began to wear on me. I started to fear that she'd leave me if I didn't give in. We often found ourselves caught up in heavy touching and kissing at each other's homes, always managing to pull back before things got out of control—but every time, my resolve felt a little weaker.

Then came a time when my girlfriend told me her father would be out of town for several days, leaving her with the house to herself. I began to convince myself that this would finally be the time I'd give in and have sex with her. But it never happened—not then, at least. Every time we were on the verge of crossing that line, my mom—who was a praying woman—would get a sense from the Holy Spirit that her son was about to do something he shouldn't. She'd call me at just the right moment and tell me to come home immediately. This went on for quite a while, and it wasn't until years later that I recognized it as my first real encounter with the Lord's faithfulness to provide an escape from temptation. The Lord was merciful, giving me chance after chance. Yet eventually, His warnings weren't enough. I ignored His gracious attempts to protect me.

One day, our school had an early dismissal due to teacher meetings, and I decided that would be the day I'd lose my virginity. I didn't tell my parents about the early release, so they assumed I'd be in school until 3:25. When the bell rang at noon, I drove to my girlfriend's house, fully committed to my decision. Out of insecurity about my lack of experience, I'd spent the entire week binge-watching porn, thinking it would prepare me for what was coming.

When we got into her room, she closed the door and told me, "I don't want to rush you, and if you're not ready or uncomfortable, we don't have to do it." And because this was something she had never told me, it made me feel safe. Yet also, it had the reverse psychological effect of making me feel like there was no way I could chicken out of it. Because I had been afraid and ashamed of going to the store and buying a condom, I told her at that moment I forgot to get a condom. And then she responded, "It's okay. I've got plenty here." It's crazy how I didn't recognize that as a major red flag then. But again, my 16-year-old brain was still developing. My girlfriend went into her closet and reached into a shoe box that she had that was full of condoms and handed me one. I'll never forget that moment when she gave me the condom, and my heart began beating out of my chest as I realized that I didn't even know what to do with the condom. Nervously, I started stuttering as she quickly understood what I was trying to say, and she told me, "Don't worry, I'll put it on for you." I was so nervous that it was hard for me to get an erection. But with some kissing and rubbing from her, once that was achieved, she put the condom on me and slowly climbed on top of me.

I asked her, "Is it in yet?"

She responded, "Yes."

As soon as she said it was in, I attempted to do exactly what I had seen in porn that week and began moving my body up and down as fast and as hard as I could. After about 30 seconds, I had ejaculated, and my erection was over. Shame immediately filled my heart and my mind as I felt like a failure due to how short this sexual experience was. I apologized to her for not being a good experience, quickly put my clothes on, and left in shame.

Driving away from her house, newly aware that I was no longer a virgin, I felt a swirl of emotions. On one hand, I felt humiliated and guilty. On the other hand, a part of me was excited to share the story with friends. Later that day, when I arrived at my job at Finish Line, I found myself bragging to my friend Bradley about having sex. I even lied, adding details about how I'd supposedly made her moan and scream, though none of it was true. I'm not sure where the impulse to lie came from, but at that point in my life, lying had become a regular habit. Even as I spun this exaggerated story, deep down, I felt grief. I knew I had let God down, and worse, I feared I'd damaged my Christian witness to my girlfriend. I worried that I'd lost the chance to show her what a man who loves Jesus and stands apart looks like, and I was afraid she might never embrace the faith I'd been praying she would find.

In the days that followed, I resolved to recommit to abstinence and vowed that I wouldn't have sex again until marriage. Though I kept that promise, my girlfriend was less pleased with my choice. She'd hoped that sex would now be a regular part of our relationship, and when she realized I was serious about abstaining, we quickly began to grow apart. She soon started seeking fulfillment elsewhere.

Looking back, though it's disappointing that I didn't enter marriage as a virgin, I'm thankful God intervened and kept me from spiraling into ongoing sexual activity. I kept my commitment to abstinence for the next ten years until I married at 26. Honoring God with my body and reminding women of their worth beyond sex became a core part of my ministry. Abstinence was incredibly challenging during my time at Howard University, where sex was readily accessible. Still, by then, God had given me strategies and supportive people to help me stay committed. I'll share those strategies in Chapter Seven, offering practical guidance on maintaining abstinence and purity. But first, I wanted to share my story as an encouragement and a caution for other men reading this book.

When I married my wife at 26, I felt deeply insecure about my lack of sexual experience. My wife, who had a past before becoming a Christian, was much more experienced, and although she never said or did anything to make me feel insecure, I was haunted by comparisons. I worried about measuring up to her past partners, both in terms of skill and physical appearance. I was afraid I might not meet some unknown standard, or worse, that my inexperience would be obvious and disappointing. I even wondered if I'd unknowingly trigger memories of her past or make her miss previous experiences.

These fears weighed heavily on me, and I struggled with the idea that I'd have to perform perfectly right away. I feared my wife would quickly realize how inexperienced I was and lose patience with me. I even questioned whether my lack of experience would make me more satisfied than her, fearing she'd be left unsatisfied and tempted to look elsewhere.

I knew these worries needed to be addressed, so as we approached marriage, I made a point to talk openly with my wife about each one. Being vulnerable about my fears lifted a weight, and I realized that sharing them reduced their power over me. My openness allowed her to understand my insecurities and reassure me of her commitment to building something new together. These conversations also paved the way for her to share her own fears—she worried I'd view her as damaged goods and felt saddened by not being able to present herself as a virgin, something she believed I deserved.

Through these honest dialogues, we both discovered that a healthy sex life in marriage is built on transparency and trust. Even though some of these fears lingered early on, over time, they faded as we continued talking openly and building intimacy. I learned that sex is 90% communication and only 10% physical. Today, I know without a doubt that none of her past experiences come close to what we share now—our emotional and physical connection is incredible because we know each other deeply, making everything else effortless.

This chapter has explored the profound ways that premarital sex can impact spiritual well-being, often straining religious beliefs and weakening the spiritual foundations that many seek to carry into marriage. In contrast, abstinence can build a firmer basis for marital happiness, as seen in the testimonies of men who waited, finding greater intimacy and trust in their relationships. My journey of insecurity around sexual inexperience compared to my wife's past experiences revealed the challenges of reconciling different histories. Yet, we fostered a deeper connection through open, honest communication, enabling me to overcome insecurities and find confidence in our shared commitment. In this way, abstinence and honest dialogue before and within marriage set the stage for lasting fulfillment—a fulfillment that I will explore further in the next chapter as we consider the unique, enduring joy that abstinence can bring to life and marriage.

CHAPTER 5:

Laying the Groundwork:
Marriage and Long-Term Happiness

I'm not sure what brought you to this book, but I do know that reading it openly is an act of courage. Just carrying this book in public signals a bold stance because its title likely stands out as strange—maybe even pointless—to most men today. The concept of abstinence might seem irrelevant and even counterproductive, especially in a culture that often views such values as outdated and restrictive. But we're living in a time when sexual purity and restraint are frequently misinterpreted as unreasonable demands from a God who supposedly wants to deny us joy. In reality, God's guidelines around sexuality—like all His commandments—are designed for our good, even if society has lost sight of this truth.

This cultural drift isn't new; we've seen it throughout history. However, today's mindset toward boundaries has grown to view them as burdensome and anyone advocating for them as oppressive or misguided. This false belief has convinced many that a life without limitations is a life of true freedom, but the truth is quite the opposite: a boundary-free life often leads to bondage. Abstinence and purity, for example, are now seen as outdated, and studies have even tried to tie our level of happiness to our sexual behavior. Yet, in pursuing greater sexual freedom, we've seen only a rise in depression, anxiety, and other signs of societal distress. Scientists often differentiate between happiness (based on circumstances) and joy (a deeper, more lasting state). However, many still suggest that by expanding our sexual freedom, we'll somehow become happier—though the evidence contradicts this.

Over the last 20 years, as sexual freedom has increased, so have mental health issues. Statistics reflect that the pursuit of autonomy in our sexual lives correlates with a decline in mental well-being. The more people abandon abstinence, the more they find themselves struggling with emotional instability, unable to form meaningful relationships. Marriage rates have plummeted, not simply because people no longer desire it, but because many can no longer commit to it. There's even an argument circulating that we weren't meant for monogamy, which is inconsistent with human biology and contradicts itself—if we can't love one person, how can we love many?

Our culture has placed autonomy on a pedestal, leading people to reject commitments of any kind, even though deep down, they often yearn for stability and unconditional love. Could our growing dissatisfaction come from going against the way we were created? Humans were made for covenant relationships, built on stable, committed love that allows us to grow and mature, flaws and all. In contrast, an unstable relationship environment only leads to a profound sense of yearning and dysfunction.

My urgent call for us to return to God's way is loud and clear. If you are a man who finds yourself depressed and emotionally unstable, yet you have not positioned yourself to commit to a covenant relationship in which both you and the person can be healed, then you are committing self-sabotage. This statement is not to say that all men must pursue marriage and are called to marriage, but instead that there needs to be a relational mindset shift in how we understand relationships in general. Even if you read this book and commit to abstinence, but apply the principles platonically to ensure that you have healthy relationships with other people in your life that hold you accountable, this world will be a much better place. But because I recognize that we live in a hypersexualized culture that looks like it has no plan on slowing down, I believe the reality is that many men would do well to rein in those sexual desires and appetites within the healthy confines of a covenantal marriage relationship.

The erosion of marriage has made it difficult for us to see the cracks in our society. Marriage was meant to demonstrate God's unwavering love for us, serving as a reminder of the beauty of love and the pain of its absence. Today, debates on sexual freedom versus abstinence rage on despite clear evidence that abstinence leads to a more fulfilled, healthier life. There are no long-term benefits to casual sexual encounters or accumulating sexual experiences. All premarital sex creates consequences and draws us away from both God and those who can help us heal. I cannot stress enough that there are no lasting benefits. If you're among those who seek immediate pleasure, I'm afraid you're choosing to learn the hard way. Satan has always deceived humanity by offering short-term gratification that hides long-term destruction. Like Adam and Eve, we will continue to eat fruit that will kill us so long as our death isn't immediate. This way of thinking has been at the helm of our human demise ever since it first happened many, many years ago in Genesis chapter 3.

As I've observed men who commit to purity and abstinence, I've noticed how their decisions impact their entire outlook on life—even beyond the realm of sexuality. Part of my motivation for writing this book is recognizing the disconnect many men experience between living fulfilling lives for God and the belief that their physical actions are separate from their beliefs. This misconception suggests that physical choices and mental convictions are unrelated. But the truth is, every action begins in the mind, and without aligning our sexual decisions with our values, we're only deceiving ourselves.

We've explored abstinence's physical and emotional effects, yet abstinence also nurtures a new way of thinking. At its core, abstinence involves principles that can produce lasting benefits when applied to other areas of life. Every natural revelation reflects a greater spiritual one. While we'll delve into the spiritual dimensions of sex in the next chapter, we'll now look at how abstinence impacts various aspects of life outside of sexuality.

Men who practice sexual discipline often exhibit greater self-control and integrity in other areas. For instance, they prioritize their health by maintaining a balanced diet and consistent exercise. They also tend to be organized and manage their time effectively, displaying productivity and commitment in their work and personal lives. Their consistent practice of personal integrity makes them dependable and morally responsible, showing respect in both professional and social settings.

Sexual discipline often translates to financial responsibility as well. Many abstinent men avoid impulsive purchases, focus on saving, and recognize the importance of financial stability for future relationships. Similarly, they cultivate emotional resilience by abstaining from casual relationships, allowing them to manage emotions more effectively and exhibit empathy in personal and professional spheres. With fewer distractions, they are more focused academically and in their careers, dedicating time and energy toward personal growth.

This commitment extends to spiritual growth. Sexual discipline is often a cornerstone for men who are serious about their faith, as it fosters the discipline required for regular prayer, Bible study, and active community involvement. Abstinent men also tend to be more socially responsible, with a deeper awareness of how their actions impact others. Many of these men invest their time in mentoring and community initiatives instead of casual relationships.

In addition, they are generally more disciplined in avoiding substance use, such as alcohol or drugs. This reflects the principle that self-control in one area can reinforce discipline in others. Lastly, abstinent men often have deeper, more authentic interpersonal relationships. Viewing friendships as essential to personal growth and accountability, they tend to engage in relationships that foster mutual respect and personal integrity.

In essence, the discipline required for abstinence frequently permeates other aspects of a man's life, shaping his approach to health, finances, relationships, and spirituality.

The Marshmallow Test, a famous experiment by psychologist Walter Mischel, offers us a striking look at the power of delayed gratification. In the experiment, young children were given a marshmallow and told they could either eat it immediately or wait for a short period to receive two marshmallows instead. The children who managed to wait demonstrated self-control, a trait Mischel's follow-up studies linked to better life outcomes years later. Those who resisted the marshmallow tended to have higher SAT scores, lower rates of substance abuse, healthier relationships, and greater success in their careers. The ability to delay gratification revealed a pattern: people who can resist immediate pleasure for the promise of a greater reward often experience more satisfaction and fulfillment in the long run.

Now, this same principle applies directly to sexual purity and abstinence. Just as the Marshmallow Test highlighted the benefits of waiting for a better outcome, abstaining from sex until marriage aligns with the idea that true rewards are worth the wait. Our culture often pushes instant gratification, especially in the realm of sexuality. We're encouraged to indulge now, to fulfill every desire without a second thought for future consequences. But like the children who ate the marshmallow right away, seeking immediate pleasure can lead to a life lacking in the deeper satisfaction and stability that come from building lasting commitments. Just as delaying gratification in the test brought about better life outcomes, so does waiting for a committed, covenantal relationship yield a richer, more meaningful intimacy.

Choosing abstinence is about exercising the same kind of self-control that children in the Marshmallow Test displayed. By holding out for something better, we cultivate patience, discipline, and an understanding that some pleasures are sweeter when delayed. Sexual intimacy, when shared within a committed marriage, brings with it an emotional and spiritual connection that casual encounters can't replicate. The world might promise us immediate pleasure, but that pleasure is often fleeting and leaves a trail of regret, insecurity, and instability. On the other hand, abstinence teaches us that true satisfaction comes from commitment, sacrifice, and the decision to invest in something enduring.

Ultimately, sexual purity and delayed gratification offer us a clearer perspective on what matters most in life. We are called to resist momentary desires and embrace a lifestyle that builds resilience, maturity, and a deeper understanding of love. The Marshmallow Test illustrates that the rewards for waiting go beyond mere marshmallows; they translate to lasting joy and fulfillment. When we apply this principle to our sexuality, we not only honor God's design for intimacy, but we also prepare ourselves for a relationship that can thrive, grounded in patience and true devotion. Like those two marshmallows, the rewards await those willing to stay the course.

While much of our focus so far has been on the explicit act of sexual intercourse, we haven't yet addressed a more pervasive challenge facing men: pornography use. Many see pornography as a safe and even virtuous substitute for premarital sex, believing that as long as they abstain from physical acts, they're avoiding harm. This mindset is common, especially among men committed to abstinence, who may convince themselves that pornography is a harmless or even healthier alternative. I once held this belief myself, rationalizing my use of pornography as a compromise that would keep me from engaging in real sexual relationships. However, I eventually realized how pornography was hindering my freedom and leading me to a distorted understanding of purity.

There were two main reasons I accepted pornography during my time practicing abstinence. First, I was influenced by flawed theological teachings that didn't address the damaging effects of pornography and underestimated God's power to help me overcome it. Second, I lacked the courage to face the truth about how pornography was corrupting my heart and leading me to sin against myself and others, much like premarital sex. I was reluctant to admit that my use of pornography was undermining my relationship with God, drawing me further away from both Him and His people. Although Chapter 7 will cover practical steps for overcoming pornography, it's essential here to shed light on its impacts. Pornography erodes a man's self-control, increasing the chances that he'll compromise his commitment to abstinence

 Why men shouldn't have sex before marriage

when facing temptation. It also affects his emotional, mental, and relational well-being, often resulting in a lower quality of life and diminished satisfaction in future marital relationships. Pornography, like premarital sex, harms relationships, leading to lower sexual satisfaction within marriage.

The secretive nature of pornography use makes it even more insidious. It's often concealed, which allows it to continue unchecked, leading to self-deception. Porn users may be unaware of how pornography erodes their sexual discipline, conditioning them to see women as objects and normalizing harmful thoughts and behaviors. In some cases, men become inundated with inappropriate and invasive sexual thoughts—even toward individuals they aren't attracted to or legally able to pursue. Moreover, numerous studies have shown that 93% of sexual and violent offenders report being avid consumers of pornography, with many attributing their crimes to pornography-induced desensitization and the eventual pursuit of real-life encounters.

Pornography can also lead men to objectify their wives, comparing them unfavorably to unrealistic portrayals they've seen online. Frequent users often report feeling isolated, experiencing difficulty forming meaningful relationships, and lacking accountability to help them achieve their goals. Beyond being a deceptive outlet, pornography distorts self-perception, convincing men that they are exercising restraint by avoiding physical acts. In reality, each viewing undermines their self-discipline, leaving them more vulnerable to temptation.

A study by the University of Windsor's psychology department in 2016 offers further insight. Researchers found that exposure to sexually explicit material lowers self-restraint and self-control. The study tested two groups—one viewing explicit material and the other non-explicit content—and discovered that those exposed to sexual material had significantly reduced self-discipline. This finding underscores that pornography directly impairs a man's ability to resist temptation, not only by eroding his sexual discipline but also by blurring his understanding of respectful and consensual relationships. As men consume more pornography, they may inadvertently internalize harmful behaviors, losing the ability to distinguish between consensual, healthy relationships and ones rooted in manipulation or control.

My experience has revealed that a profound shift often occurs in abstinent men, where they begin prioritizing and being intentional about the relationships they build. This shift typically accompanies sexual discipline for several reasons. One primary reason is that when a man is not pursuing sex, he engages in deeper emotional and relational conversations with his partner. This clarity makes him more aware that his partner is not an object but a person. By seeing his partner without the cloudiness of sex, he can make a more objective assessment of her character, strengths, and flaws. Through this, he begins to realize that no matter how great his partner is, she can't provide all the emotional and relational support he'll need throughout his life.

This awareness often leads him to seek out additional friendships that offer what his partner may lack. This differs from men who are sexually active outside of marriage, as they often live under the illusion that they and their partner are self-sufficient on an island, needing no one else. While not all sexually active men believe this, those without the responsibility of emotional availability are more susceptible to it. Unfortunately, these men face a rude awakening when the infatuation period fades or they encounter their first challenging season in marriage. Men who lack the support of deep interpersonal relationships during such times can struggle the most. Those who expect their partner to fulfill all their emotional needs apply pressure that ultimately risks breaking her down over time.

My wife and I have made it a priority to spend time with friends who bring life, encouragement, and strength to our marriage. While we have criteria for these friends shaped by our marital relationship, one primary criterion is that they encourage us to turn toward each other in times of conflict. Often, time with a friend equips me to love, serve, and support my wife better. Many men are unaware of the effort it takes to be gentle, loving, and caring as a husband—mainly because our culture hasn't promoted this image or provided models for how to begin. In the safety of these friendships, I discuss aspects of life that may be more complex or difficult for my wife to understand. For clarity, these relationships don't replace what I bring to her but complement it.

Some men believe that not every issue should be shared with their spouse, discerning which matters she can handle. However, I've observed that secrecy under any guise, even with good intentions, can create a wedge between partners that fosters disunity. While sensitivity to time and place is crucial when sharing difficult matters, learning to communicate openly with a spouse is a skill that must be developed. In marriage, the goal should be to return to the original state of Adam and Eve: completely naked and unashamed before one another.

Abstinence can restore face-to-face communication in a world where so much is conducted over mobile devices and online. Abstinent men value honest, face-to-face conversations with their partner and others, understanding the power of healthy dialogue. These men are also more likely to maintain close ties with family and friends because they're not emotionally distracted by sex's hormonal shifts. They can better incorporate their family into the relationship-building process without neglecting important relationships. This approach contributes to a supportive village to help them navigate relationships, providing a safe place for accountability and growth.

Conversely, men who cut off meaningful relationships once they find a significant other miss out on these benefits. Abstinent men often foster deep, fulfilling friendships that serve as safe havens, helping them avoid losing themselves and empowering them to bring their best selves into their relationship. Friends and family who knew them before their romantic relationships can play a vital role in keeping them grounded, enabling them to maintain their individuality even within a partnership.

The third significant ideological shift for a man pursuing abstinence is the strengthening of his commitment to his personal beliefs. Abstinence, by nature, demands both offensive and defensive action—a continual work of resisting temptation and avoiding compromising situations. While it may appear straightforward, abstinence requires intense mental fortitude, forward-thinking, and meticulous planning of each day. Over time, this diligence doesn't just reshape a man's thoughts and desires; it lays the foundation for a deeper conviction as he witnesses God's power and faithfulness in his life. Every abstinent man reaches a breaking point where he realizes he can't sustain this journey alone. Whether he's challenged by a woman inviting him to have sex or faces ridicule from other men, this moment inevitably arrives. Those who press through this struggle experience a transformation unique to the discipline of abstinence.

I remember this exact moment at Howard University. I had just declined an opportunity to be with a woman who was practically throwing herself at me. After nearly three years of abstinence, I felt isolated in a world where college men lived freely and indulgently. Word of my commitment had spread around campus. While not everyone was against my choice, my abstinence triggered two discomforts in others: it convicted those who understood the importance of my decision and threatened the men around me, who feared guilt by association. This isolation brought me to a place of desperation, where I realized that without God's answers for the benefits of abstinence, I might abandon my resolve and join the crowd.

Surrounded by a culture that declared college as the time to explore sexual freedom without consequence, I constantly wondered if I was missing out. Every bold move I made was met with internal questioning and external pressure from men around me who had no qualms about living without conviction. Hitting this wall was profound because it forced me to confront whether I was abstinent only for the benefits or if I was truly committed to a higher purpose beyond immediate outcomes. My commitment to abstinence ultimately solidified my commitment to God.

As a young man raised in a Christian home, my life decisions had always been guided by the beliefs of others. This journey, however, revealed to me the danger of living by someone else's convictions. A man cannot sustain abstinence on borrowed beliefs; genuine commitment must stem from his own deeply held values. My father had always taught me to make decisions from a place of conviction, not convenience. He said he'd never be upset by a choice I made that contradicted his guidance, but he would be disappointed if I made that choice simply because everyone else was doing it. In enduring the ridicule of others, I emerged stronger, more confident, and more secure in my beliefs.

Through my experiences and conversations with other men on this journey, I've seen that around the second or third year of abstinence, most men encounter a similar crossroad. For me, it happened after a woman attempted to seduce me in my dorm room, reminiscent of the story of Joseph in the Bible. This encounter forced me to assess my commitment and decide if abstinence was truly my path.

One truth remains: I've never met a man who wasn't richly rewarded after obediently following the call of abstinence from God. There's no such example. You won't find a man who has chosen abstinence and hasn't reaped the benefits a hundredfold. Standing firm in my conviction as a college freshman was when my beliefs became my own, and I began to secure future blessings. At the time, I couldn't foresee the rewards; it would take nearly eight years to understand the full extent of God's provision. But obedience works that way—our rewards are revealed only after we commit to the path. This kind of faith isn't for everyone; it demands a trust in God that few are willing to embrace, especially when the rewards are often delayed and beyond our control.

But in the crucible of testing, where a man's understanding and patience are stretched, his character is fortified. Though each man's reward is unique, for me, turning down that woman led to the supernatural strength to resist sexual temptation, conquer pornography, and practice self-control. This strength would continue to grow with each act of obedience in my life. That initial test of trusting God, despite not understanding the total outcome, marked the beginning of my journey into deeper conviction. When I stepped back and reflected on that moment, I realized I could never doubt Jesus again. He had shown me His power by granting me self-control that could only come from Him.

Obedience is about surrendering to God's will and trusting that His ways are higher than ours. While the rewards may differ from what we expect, they are always worth the wait. In a later chapter, we'll explore how obedience doesn't guarantee specific blessings but rather invites God's perfect provision. Often, I've

 Why men shouldn't have sex before marriage

expected rewards from God based on my obedience, only to learn that I can't dictate the terms of His blessings. Yet, every sacrifice has made me more resilient and rooted in faith.

For a man who perseveres through this journey of abstinence, he emerges from the fire refined—stronger, wiser, and more secure. In saying "no" to temptation, I tangibly experienced God's power. The realization that I could resist what my body craved confirmed God's strength within me, an assurance I carry to this day.

Reflecting on my abstinence journey, I realize how integral it's been to my love and appreciation for the church and the faith community. Without the commitment to a life of purity over the past decade, I doubt I'd feel this same depth of connection. The fourth way abstinence shapes a man's philosophy is by cultivating a deep appreciation for meaningful connections. Living counterculturally highlights the importance of camaraderie and community, and it quickly became apparent which relationships supported or challenged my journey. When spending time with friends who were sexually active, I often found myself in uncomfortable situations, feeling pressured or ridiculed for my choices. I soon learned which groups encouraged purity not just in action but in thought as well. Abstinence requires purifying the mind, a process influenced heavily by the conversations and interactions we experience daily. As I became more aware of my friends' influence on my commitment to purity, I grew increasingly grateful for those whose presence aligned with my goals. Time spent with such friends was like a refreshing drink after wandering in a desert.

My college experience was a blessing because it didn't isolate me from others with different values. Instead, it forced me to navigate a world that doesn't always share my convictions, teaching me how to engage lovingly with others while protecting my own beliefs. I didn't live in a "purity bubble," shielded from the realities of those with different lifestyles. I hope that every man pursuing purity will find this balance. Real discipline isn't built in the absence of temptation but within its very crucible. Many men live abstinently because their circumstances limit temptation, but true strength develops through repeated opportunities to resist and grow.

In college, I discovered that like-minded men tend to form strong communities bound by mutual support and accountability. When I found other abstinent men, I quickly became connected to entire networks where we encouraged one another. As I came to realize how powerful these communities were, I also noticed the societal pressure that often silences men who are committed to abstinence. These men—myself included—have faced ridicule and criticism when openly sharing our convictions. I believe this silence is part of a spiritual attack, limiting the influence of our testimonies. Many men accept society's narrative about sexuality simply because they don't know an alternative exists. As the saying goes, "A man cannot become what he has not seen." In a world where men committed to purity are silent, it's no surprise others struggle to imagine a different path.

My frustration is that many abstinent men only share their testimonies after they marry, proclaiming, "I did it!" While inspiring, these stories miss the power they would have held if shared in the midst of the journey, showing others that it's possible to thrive even in the face of temptation. For many men, the lack of visible role models fosters a belief that all men are at the mercy of their desires. Imagine a millionaire living in poverty but never revealing his wealth; while it might shield him from particular challenges, it robs his neighbors of hope for a different future. This is why I'm passionate about calling men to not only embrace sexual purity but also to be vocal about it. By sharing their convictions, they foster accountability and provide a beacon for others to follow.

Ultimately, pursuing purity is strengthened by community. These connections don't just keep us on track; they help others see that an alternative path is possible and worth pursuing.

The fifth way abstinence benefits men is by helping them define and understand their purpose more clearly. Through the discipline of abstinence—which is often rooted in recognizing its long-term benefits for marriage and emotional well-being—men learn to evaluate the broader impact of their decisions. By choosing to abstain, these men reject distractions that could pull them away from their purpose. All of the abstinent men I know who waited until marriage discovered their calling at a younger age. Their clarity in life came from the fact that their time and mental energy weren't compromised by casual sexual relationships.

Because these men regularly engaged in spiritual activities, like Bible study and being part of a faith community, they were often led to consider the lasting impact they wanted to have. In contrast, men who become sexually active at a young age and maintain casual relationships can struggle to find purpose. Premarital sex can cloud our direction, offering temporary fulfillment that deters us from pursuing something deeper. Research also supports this: men who were less sexually active tended to choose careers with a more substantial impact, especially on the next generation. In contrast, those who became sexually active earlier often ended up in task-oriented or labor-focused roles.

This correlation suggests that men who guard their sexual health also develop a mindset oriented toward others. Additionally, studies show that men who were abstinent early on tend to have more stability in their careers. As men are leaving home and becoming independent later than in previous generations, statistics highlight that those who did so earlier—moving out, marrying, and fully supporting themselves—were often the ones who practiced abstinence during their teenage years.

These trends underscore the influence of abstinence on life choices and the early realization of a man's career and life goals. In fact, before the 1960s—when monogamous, nonsexual relationships were more common—men were more financially independent at younger ages and lived more stable adult lives. At a time when many are seeking meaningful and stable careers, studies indicate that men who pursue abstinence often find purpose sooner and experience greater fulfillment in their chosen paths.

I'm sure it's no secret by now that I'm a Christian, and my belief that men should embrace abstinence comes deeply from my Christian convictions. But it's important to recognize that Christianity is not alone in this view. Other religions, such as Islam and Judaism, also uphold abstinence as a fundamental principle. These faith traditions value abstinence because they have a deep respect and reverence for the human body and see it as a way to honor their Creator. In these religions, casual sexual relationships outside of marriage are believed to be not only disrespectful to God but also disruptive to a thriving society.

The doctrines in these faiths, rooted in their sacred texts, advocate abstinence as a way to honor oneself and one's future spouse and as a divine command. Various interpretations of their holy books emphasize that abstinence promotes emotional and physical well-being while aligning with divine purpose.

When we expand our view beyond religious perspectives, we also find non-religious philosophies that support abstinence for ethical and philosophical reasons. There are secular worldviews with no connection to a divine being that recognizes the importance of restraint in matters of sex, drawing on concepts of metaphysics, ethics, and responsibility. For example, Immanuel Kant's philosophy emphasizes treating others as ends in themselves, not merely as means to an end, which applies strongly to sexual relationships. This view fosters a sense of responsibility and intentionality in one's sexual choices.

In addition to Kant, other non-religious philosophies have also advocated for self-restraint. Stoic thinkers like Epictetus and Seneca emphasized self-control as a pathway to inner peace, teaching that excessive pleasure-seeking disrupts one's ability to live virtuously. Stoicism promotes discipline over impulses, viewing restraint as essential for personal and societal well-being.

Existentialism, though often associated with personal freedom, includes thinkers like Simone de Beauvoir, who argued that abstaining from sex or managing sexual relationships thoughtfully helps individuals maintain authenticity and autonomy. Existentialists believe that meaning comes from deliberate choices rather than succumbing to fleeting desires.

Even within Humanism, there's an understanding of the value of responsible sexual behavior. While Humanism doesn't directly promote abstinence, it does encourage actions that benefit humanity and emphasizes the importance of intentional, respectful relationships. Many humanists advocate for sexual relationships based on genuine connection, which can lead some to promote abstinence or long-term monogamy in certain contexts to avoid harm or exploitation.

These secular philosophies offer perspectives on self-restraint and sexual ethics outside of any religious framework, focusing instead on personal development, discipline, and the societal impact of one's actions.

Beyond religious and philosophical ideologies, people advocate for abstinence for various reasons, many of which are deeply rooted in community and family values. Traditional practices and social norms continue to thrive across different regions of the world, particularly in developing countries with limited access to technology. In these contexts, abstinence is often viewed as a means of honoring cultural and social values that dictate acceptable behavior and uphold reputations within the community.

While religious beliefs often intertwine with these cultural influences, some groups embrace abstinence purely because it aligns with their societal norms. In many cases, individuals who deviate from these traditions risk social exile, severe punishment, or even violence. In various societies, abstinence promotes social order, preserves family integrity, and maintains strategic familial alliances.

For instance, among Haitian and Haitian-American communities, abstinence until marriage is a prevalent cultural norm closely linked to concepts of family honor and respectability. This cultural framework can exist independently of religious teachings, even in secular environments.

Similarly, in Japan, younger generations increasingly delay marriage and sexual activity. Factors like social pressures, economic challenges, and a desire for personal independence contribute to this trend, leading many to prioritize career development and personal growth over traditional relationship milestones.

Various Indigenous cultures also emphasize sexual restraint as part of their community values, often driven by social norms surrounding marriage and family. In these cases, the emphasis on abstinence is more about maintaining social order than adhering to religious beliefs.

In Western contexts, particularly among younger adults identifying as "nones" (those with no religious affiliation), there is a growing trend toward delaying sexual activity. Many in this demographic seek deeper emotional connections and personal growth, rejecting societal pressures to engage in sexual relationships.

These examples demonstrate that cultural values and social dynamics significantly shape views on abstinence, often independent of religious or philosophical frameworks.

Additionally, for those who think abstinence is solely the domain of religious or traditionally minded individuals, there's another perspective: scientists and psychologists have conducted extensive research highlighting the benefits of abstinence. Their studies reveal statistical data comparing those who choose abstinence with those who engage in sexual activity. Research indicates that bonding hormones like oxytocin and vasopressin, which are released during sex, can complicate future emotional connections. Those involved in casual sexual relationships often experience hormonal imbalances that hinder effective bonding with future partners.

Moreover, evidence suggests that individuals with fewer sexual encounters tend to enjoy better mental well-being and experience fewer stress-related health issues. Among psychologists and health scientists, there's a growing movement advocating for lifestyles of purity, motivated by research demonstrating its long-term benefits for overall well-being.

Together, these religious, philosophical, cultural, and psychological factors create a compelling case for the assertion that premarital sex can be costly and that abstinence offers societal benefits.

The contrast between the empowerment often associated with sexual freedom and the fulfillment derived from practicing abstinence and self-control is a complex and nuanced topic. Many contemporary cultural narratives celebrate sexual freedom as a pathway to personal liberation, self-expression, and autonomy. This perspective is rooted in the belief that engaging in sexual activity can lead to empowerment, enhanced confidence, and deeper intimacy. Proponents argue that sexual freedom allows individuals to explore their desires without societal constraints, promoting a sense of agency and ownership over their bodies and choices.

However, this celebration of sexual freedom often overlooks the potential downsides of casual sexual relationships, such as emotional detachment, increased anxiety, and feelings of emptiness. Studies have shown that individuals engaging in frequent casual sexual encounters may experience negative psychological effects, including lower relationship satisfaction and heightened feelings of loneliness. Moreover, the pursuit of sexual freedom can lead to situations where individuals may feel pressured to conform to societal norms surrounding sexual activity, ultimately compromising their true desires and values.

In contrast, practicing abstinence and self-control is associated with a different kind of empowerment that emphasizes personal growth, emotional stability, and meaningful relationships. Many who choose abstinence cite a sense of fulfillment that comes from aligning their actions with their values, often resulting in stronger emotional bonds and a deeper appreciation for intimacy when it occurs within a committed relationship. Abstinence can foster a sense of discipline and self-respect, allowing individuals to prioritize their emotional and mental well-being over immediate gratification.

Research has indicated that those who practice abstinence may experience better mental health outcomes, as they often report lower levels of stress, anxiety, and depression compared to their sexually active peers. Furthermore, the commitment to self-control can lead to a more profound sense of purpose and direction in life, reinforcing the belief that true empowerment comes from self-discipline rather than the mere act of engaging in sexual relationships.

One man I interviewed explained how abstinence shaped his marriage, particularly in terms of conflict resolution. He shared that his commitment to remaining pure before marriage helped shift the foundation of his relationship toward deeper communication. By abstaining from physical intimacy, he and his wife were able to focus on building a solid friendship, truly getting to know one another, and understanding each other's conflict resolution styles. He emphasized that, without the influence of sexual intimacy, they had the space to tackle various relational challenges early on, giving them valuable "reps" in communication. As he put it, they weren't distracted by the physical aspect; instead, they were consistently engaging in meaningful conversations that likely wouldn't have occurred if sex had been a factor. This period of abstinence allowed them to strengthen their relationship in ways that continue to positively impact their ability to work through conflicts together.

Another man I interviewed echoed a similar sentiment to further support the connection between abstinence and deeper relational fulfillment. He emphasized that because he and his wife built their relationship on a genuine friendship without the influence of sex, they were more committed to understanding each other when conflicts arose. He explained that, in relationships where sex occurs before marriage, especially when it's casual, the foundation often shifts away from true friendship to being focused on physical intimacy. This lack of a solid relational base can make it harder to navigate conflict because the couple hasn't developed the emotional skills or "muscles" necessary to work through issues. In his experience, sexual relationships tend to prioritize personal gratification, so when the partner is no longer satisfying or becomes too much to deal with, people can more easily move on. But in a friendship-based relationship, there is a deeper focus on the other person as a whole rather than just seeing them as someone who fulfills sexual desires. This perspective reinforces the idea that abstinence allows for the development of a stronger emotional foundation, which is critical for handling conflict and nurturing a long-lasting relationship.

To provide a contrasting perspective, another man I interviewed shared how his relationship was affected by an early focus on sex, which led to significant challenges once he and his partner married. He admitted that they "did things backward," quickly beginning a sexual relationship that became a central part of their connection. The physical intimacy, though enjoyable, inadvertently prevented them from having crucial conversations and dealing with disagreements as they arose. Instead, they often took trips together to ignore unresolved issues, trips that inevitably included sexual intimacy. This cycle of avoidance allowed big problems to fester, and they fell into a pattern of ignoring each other for periods before resuming contact without addressing their underlying issues.

After marriage, however, they found they could no longer escape these conflicts, and issues they hadn't previously acknowledged began to surface. The strain nearly led to divorce shortly after their wedding, but thanks to some honest input from other couples, they realized they had skipped the vital step of building a friendship. These couples pointed out that their attraction had clouded their judgment, making them believe they were in love when they were only physically attracted. Now, with guidance, they are learning to communicate, build friendship, and foster the kind of connection that sustains a marriage. He reflected on how much they both wish they had understood the dangers of premarital sex and how it can create a false sense of intimacy that, once removed, leaves significant gaps to fill in a marriage.

The findings from the Dunedin Multidisciplinary Health and Development Study provide compelling evidence of the profound benefits of self-control for long-term well-being and fulfillment. This longitudinal study, which tracked over 1,000 individuals from birth into adulthood, highlighted how early self-control is a powerful predictor of adult success, encompassing health, financial stability, and social success. Remarkably, this relationship held across socioeconomic backgrounds and intelligence levels, showing that self-control is a universally beneficial trait that transcends other variables. When applied to a lifestyle of abstinence, which is inherently a form of self-control, the data suggests that men who practice abstinence may reap similar health, happiness, and life satisfaction benefits.

The study's findings on life satisfaction underscore the connection between self-control and fulfillment. Individuals with high self-control were much more likely to report satisfaction with their lives, with 90% of those scoring highest in self-control assessments expressing overall life contentment. In contrast, those with lower self-control not only reported lower life satisfaction but also faced a higher risk of mental health challenges, with 22% of the bottom fifth in self-control scores attempting or committing suicide by age 38. In comparison, only 7% of those with high self-control made similar attempts. This significant disparity reveals that self-control predicts practical success and is intimately tied to psychological well-being. Abstinence, as a form of self-discipline, reinforces self-control in a man's life and can lead to these same positive outcomes. By mastering self-control in the realm of sexuality, men often find they can extend this skill to other areas of life, experiencing greater stability, purpose, and resilience.

For young men, developing self-control early on, particularly in relation to sexual behavior, is critical. Abstinence serves as a training ground for self-control, shaping men into individuals capable of maintaining boundaries and prioritizing long-term goals over immediate gratification. As the study suggests, the habits formed in childhood and adolescence often continue into adulthood, highlighting the importance of instilling values like abstinence before unhealthy sexual habits have a chance to take root. When men are taught to value abstinence as part of a larger framework of self-discipline, they are not just preparing themselves to avoid immediate temptations but laying the groundwork for a more fulfilling life in all areas.

Furthermore, while many believe self-control is difficult to cultivate beyond a certain age, this perspective overlooks the transformative power of a spiritual relationship with God. Through a spiritual conversion and the influence of the Holy Spirit, many men discover a newfound motivation to pursue purity and self-control. This spiritual dimension is key: when men choose abstinence as a response to a loving and forgiving God, they are empowered to live a lifestyle that aligns with their beliefs. This connection between faith and self-control can produce a level of fulfillment that goes beyond what mere willpower can accomplish. True abstinence, when pursued with an understanding of God's unconditional love, yields profound personal growth and satisfaction that aligns with the study's findings on the benefits of self-control.

One of my favorite phrases in life is the biblical statement, "Wisdom is proved by its results." I believe this statement is often underestimated for how truthful it is and the kind of guide it can be when we are learning from the mistakes of others and trying to determine which decisions make sense for our lives. In our conversation about premarital sex, many people swear their way of doing relationships is the best way. Yet, they are unwilling to face the results that others have proclaimed before their very eyes. They hear warning after warning about the results of premarital sex and how it opposes a life of fulfillment. Yet, they somehow believe that they will be the one person in the history of the world to get a different outcome. Not only is this pride, but it is also pure foolishness—especially when men have gone out of their way to be honest and vulnerable enough to share their painful experiences in a book like this. Let's examine the results and see what some virgin men had to say about how remaining a virgin benefitted their marriage. Afterward, we'll hear from some more men about how they wish they would've waited.

A man who waited until marriage to have sex described how abstinence helped lay a strong foundation for his relationship, further proving that "wisdom is proved by its results." He shared that because neither he nor his wife had prior sexual experiences, they had "nothing to compare each other to" and no room for pride. Both started from "square zero," learning together, making mistakes, and discovering what worked for each other. This mutual vulnerability cultivated a unique humility between them and a sense of safety and security that has allowed their marriage to flourish. He said, "We can fully be ourselves and don't have to walk around worrying about cheating on each other, not being ourselves, or being awkward." He acknowledged that while challenges still exist, abstinence closed the door to certain insecurities, creating a marriage where they could be open and genuine with one another. For him, the results of this commitment reveal the wisdom in their choice, providing a depth of intimacy and trust that continues to strengthen their bond.

Inversely, a man I interviewed who was sexually active before marriage expressed regret over not waiting. He reflected, "Neither of us were virgins, and it would've been beneficial for both of us to wait until marriage because it would've made it more special between us. My wife even had a kid from a previous relationship when we got together. If we had waited, it would've been all we knew, and we would've had nothing else to compare each other to." He added that this lack of comparison was something he longed for, admitting that it had been "a big initial challenge" for him. His perspective reinforces the idea that experiences before marriage can sometimes introduce complexities and challenges that abstinence might avoid.

One of the things that I hypothesized at the beginning of writing this book was that couples who were abstinent before marriage would have less conflict than those who were sexually active before marriage. I also hypothesized that the sources of their marital conflicts would also be different. My research did not confirm my hypothesis, as sexual history appeared to show no clear correlation between the frequency or nature of a couple's conflicts. Despite being unable to draw a clear correlation, there seems to be a sense that couples naturally progress through types of conflict depending on how long they've been married. For example, newly married couples tend to argue about chores, routine, and responsibilities, while couples that were married longer often emphasize it less. Couples that are new parents with one or two children tend to argue about parenting and getting on the same page. All couples seem to argue intensely and often, and healthier couples argue the most. This signifies their desire to be honest enough to confront one another and their security and safety to speak their minds honestly.

was able to draw a clear conclusion that couples who had waited to have sex before marriage all had marriages that were supported by either therapists or mentor couples. Only a few couples that had been sexually active before marriage utilized therapy or mentor couples.

With all of the many things we have talked about in this chapter, the common thread has been fulfillment and the way that premarital sex robs men of this reality. Many people have their own reasons for choosing to live abstinent, and it is not a decision that is only reserved for religious or traditional people. The research is abundantly clear, and more and more people are waking up to the truth that sexual freedom and autonomy do not actually lead to a more fulfilled life but rather to a larger group of problems that ultimately lead to death. Suppose you have hesitated about abstaining because you are not religious or traditional. In that case, I hope this chapter has thoroughly exposed you to the reality that abstinence extends to more expansive groups than just the usual two. As the research continues to show that abstinent people hardly regret their decision, it is a powerful time for you to consider making a life change for yourself and the others around you. And if you have already been living an abstinent lifestyle up to this point, I hope you are inspired and motivated to continue. As I've briefly touched on the spiritual implications of premarital sex, let's dive deep into the aspects of sex that most people are unaware of in the next chapter.

CHAPTER 6:

A Sacred Act:
The Spiritual Dimension of Sex

From a spiritual perspective, the discussion around sex becomes layered and significant. We live in a world where the physical is deeply connected to the spiritual—where what we can see and touch is often a reflection of an unseen realm that is more real than what we perceive. Sex is no exception. Although we are bombarded with physical representations of sex—focused on body types, appearance, and physical acts—the spiritual aspect of sex is what gives it profound power and potential danger. This understanding is not unique to Christianity; many ancient cultures and belief systems also held that sex was deeply spiritual. This concept is as old as humanity itself.

The Bible references ancient nations around Israel that incorporated sex into their worship, reflecting their belief that sex was a means of connecting with their gods. For example, ancient Mesopotamian cultures used ritualistic sexual practices to honor their deities. This historical context highlights how

 Why men shouldn't have sex before marriage

ancient peoples understood sex as more than a physical act—it was a way of seeking divine favor or spiritual union. Israel was commanded to reject these practices, even though such customs were common among their neighbors. The command set Israel apart, forbidding them from engaging in sexual acts as forms of worship, as other nations did. Though surrounded by societies that used sacred or everyday items to worship their gods, Israel was to maintain a distinct form of worship, one that did not include sex as an offering to the divine.

In many ancient cultures, such as those in Egypt and Canaan, people believed that sex with multiple partners could please their gods, which often led to orgiastic rituals. Fertility practices aimed at securing successful pregnancies also became widespread. Additionally, some cultures revered their leaders as divine; for example, Egyptian pharaohs were considered gods in human form, and sex with them was thought to bring blessings to entire communities. These societies often had hierarchical structures in which kings and wealthy leaders embraced polyamorous or polygamous relationships, viewing sexual gratification as a privilege that was never to be denied.

Moreover, these practices reinforced patriarchal systems where women existed mainly to please men. In such societies, women were often treated as property, with wives and servant-girls alike expected to serve the sexual desires of their husbands or masters. Although the Bible recounts such practices among Israel's neighbors, it also tells of Israel's frequent failure to remain distinct. Despite God's clear command to live differently, Israel repeatedly fell into the same idolatrous and sexually charged rituals that other nations practiced, actions that God condemned and called sinful.

Throughout scripture, it's clear that God sees sex as sacred, using the nations surrounding Israel to instruct His people in unexpected ways. While many read the Bible assuming that Israel serves as the exemplary nation, it's often the reverse. Possessing God's law, prophets, and direct guidance, Israel is expected to uphold a higher standard. Ironically, when God or His representatives confront these hypersexualized and idolatrous Gentile nations, they are often more willing to repent and abandon their pagan practices. In contrast, Israel, who "knows better" and has clear instructions from God, frequently hardens its heart, resisting its own prophets and repeatedly turning to idolatry. The Bible often portrays Israel as an example of what not to do, illustrating how quickly they fall into the very behaviors God commands them to avoid. This contrast underscores that while sex is inherently spiritual and meant to honor God, it becomes dangerous and destructive when used in ways that disregard God's intended purpose for it. It also emphasizes the importance of being truly repentant and responsive to God rather than stubbornly clinging to practices that lead away from Him.

As I touched on earlier, one of the themes that has always fascinated me is how strongly the Bible—especially the wisdom found in Proverbs—warns men against falling into the trap of a promiscuous woman. The repeated—almost insistent—caution highlights how this path has led to the downfall of many great men and that those who go down this road often do not return. This underscores the fact that sex has long been one of the most significant forces capable of altering a man's life. We've already looked at how men's lives can change drastically in areas like finances, careers, or even academics due to sexual choices. On a spiritual level, the Bible suggests that great men with significant influence, power, and anointing often experience a shift in their spiritual state when they fall into sexual sin.

In Proverbs, we consistently see references to men who know they should avoid these women yet allow themselves to flirt with temptation, as if they believe they can look but not touch. This brings a fresh perspective to scriptures like "flee sexual immorality," especially when we consider stories like that of Joseph, who fled Potiphar's wife so quickly that he left his garment in her hand. The Bible makes it clear that the only proper response to sexual temptation is to flee; any man who tries to fight it will ultimately fail.

The recurring moral failures of influential men throughout history, especially those in religious roles, seem to confirm this reality. For instance, when a pastor is exposed for corruption or moral failure, it's almost always assumed to be sexual in nature—and more often than not, it is. This pattern is well-known and raises questions for a watching world that wants to see men of integrity who hold to the convictions they preach. Yet, it seems that a spiritual darkness surrounding sexual sin ensnares men who initially have the potential and desire to live righteous lives.

This suggests a more profound truth: sexual compromise often indicates a broader spiritual and internal compromise. Many theologians have noted the Bible's frequent metaphor of Israel as an unfaithful spouse, equating adultery with idolatry. Adultery is idolatry in the natural realm, just as idolatry is adultery in the spiritual realm. When something in a man's life takes the place of God, it becomes both his idol and his lover—not in that it loves him, but in that it becomes the object of his misplaced affection, drawing him away from God, who jealously calls him back.

If adultery represents idolatry fully grown, then sex becomes a spiritual litmus test of where a man's heart truly lies. I knew I was meant to write this book because I began to see entire generations of men not only succumbing to sexual sin but unaware that their spiritual desires were connected to their physical obedience and submission to God. There is no separation between what we believe about God and how we live out those beliefs. Our decisions with our bodies are some of the most precise indicators of where our hearts pledge allegiance.

For men who bear witness to God's goodness, sexual sin should not only be something to resist actively but also a tangible measure of where their hearts are. Even Jesus' temptation in the wilderness illustrates this; when Satan tempted Him to turn stones into bread, it wasn't an evil act in itself, but it was outside of God's plan for Jesus. Satan often tempts men to gain good things, like sex, in ways that go against God's will and timing.

Similarly, I've watched respected men fall from their positions due to sexual sin, and I've become convinced that these failures are seldom the initial compromise. Before the act of premarital or extramarital sex, a man's heart may have already become hardened by disregarding smaller convictions. For example, a man who once guarded his eyes diligently might begin to rationalize subtle lapses, partly due to the lack of accountability around him. Over time, he may allow lingering gazes to evolve into suggestive compliments, all under the guise of "encouragement," until, without realizing it, he's drifted far from his initial standards.

These small compromises add up, eventually leading to situations that one would never choose in a sober moment. This is the progressive nature of sin, often revealed in men who eventually experience public disgrace. Satan takes his time, waiting to expose men at their weakest, amplifying the narrative that no one can truly uphold Christian values. In a world quick to focus on external sin, we must reconnect the spiritual with the physical reality. Idolatry—replacing God with anything or anyone—is synonymous with adultery. If left unchecked, this heart condition will lead to manifest acts of idolatry in our lives.

 Why men shouldn't have sex before marriage

We often view fallen men with a sense of arrogance, as though we are above such weakness. But we are all susceptible to idolatry, a sin that leads naturally to physical compromise. This brings to light a deeper spiritual connection that occurs during sex. While the physical effects are well-documented, there is also a spiritual dynamic. Men often adopt aspects of the spiritual condition of the women they engage with, a phenomenon frequently referred to as "soul ties." In the Bible, we see examples of this in the stories of Dinah and Tamar, where strong, often unpredictable emotions followed sexual encounters.

God instructed Israel not to intermarry with other nations to prevent them from adopting the spiritual dispositions of those around them. Sexual relations outside of marriage put a man at risk of bonding spiritually with someone who may not share his faith. A man solid in his faith places that faith at risk when he casually engages in sexual relationships, often manifesting in disloyalty to God.

God's jealous love will not allow us to place another on His throne. This separation from God's will brings both spiritual and natural consequences. I'm reminded of a conversation with a friend whose mentor, a pastor, confessed that after entering into an affair, he felt the tangible loss of God's presence. It wasn't until years later, after repenting, that he felt God's favor return. This loss was due to his disobedience and lack of integrity, costing him years of his life and hindering his ministry.

Many men avoid admitting that their lives lack fruitfulness due to their disobedience and sexual sin. But to be vigilant, we must guard our hearts and bodies, refusing to compromise our allegiance to God. This vigilance reminds us that our faith must be evident in both our hearts and actions.

An essential aspect of sex and its spiritual significance is that the physical pleasure of sex must be intimately connected to its procreative intention. Unfortunately, society and culture have separated these two aspects, promoting radical extremes that glorify sex either as purely for pleasure or solely for procreation. While both are true, they must remain intertwined to grasp the spiritual purpose of sex. In many ways, purity culture has mirrored the world by clinging to these polarized extremes instead of unifying these crucial aspects.

Today's culture has predominantly adopted the view that sex is purely for pleasure. As a result, society has worked hard to eliminate the connection to procreation and avoid the responsibilities of parenthood if pregnancy occurs. This manifests in the booming industry of contraception, from condoms to birth control and even abortion. By promoting this extreme, the culture perpetuates the lie that sex is merely recreational, where conception should be avoided or downplayed. This has led to a world where sex has been divorced from committed relationships, with people selectively focusing on the pleasurable aspects that reinforce this narrative.

Conversely, many religious organizations and purity movements have gone to great lengths to strip the concept of pleasure from sex, presenting it solely as a procreative act. This approach has caused many to believe the lie that sex is inherently evil or shameful, with no room for enjoyment. Such teaching has fostered legalistic mindsets, and ironically, it has led to hidden sexual fetishes. Recent studies show that purity culture has sometimes increased premarital sex rates by instilling an intense curiosity through its negative portrayals of sex. This aligns with 1 Corinthians, where the Bible says that "the law is the strength of sin." Essentially, a legalistic or rule-bound mindset often backfires, fueling the very behaviors it aims to control.

 Why men shouldn't have sex before marriage

This underscores why it's crucial to reshape our thinking and teaching on sex, affirming that it is both good and a gift from God. Many parents, by incessantly nagging their children about sex in purely negative terms, have unwittingly pushed them toward promiscuity. Freedom can be found in embracing the reality that sex is both for pleasure and procreation, and these aspects aren't competing but rather complement each other. This balanced view enables us to understand the context in which sex should occur—a covenantal relationship—while freeing us from guilt and shame. It allows couples to enjoy sex within a committed relationship that provides a stable environment for children to flourish.

Research overwhelmingly shows that children born into stable homes with married parents tend to have more successful lives than those born into single-parent homes. Although data varies depending on whether those parents remain married, it's still clear that covenantal marriage provides tremendous benefits for children.

Restoring a healthy framework for sex empowers married couples to openly share the blessings of their sexual relationship, modeling a fulfilling marriage to others. Sex and love are topics that consistently draw interest and investment. Yet, those who thrive in their marriages often remain silent due to a church culture that avoids associating sex with pleasure. This silence drives children to learn about sex from strangers online, pornography, or their peers—sources not committed to a biblical framework and often devoid of truth that could protect them. Instead, parents should be their children's trusted guides, talking openly about sex in a loving, honest manner that prepares them for a healthy view of sexuality grounded in faith and truth.

Genesis chapter 3 is the well-known story of Adam and Eve being deceived by the serpent into eating the fruit that God commanded them not to eat. This act of disobedience set off a chain reaction, explaining why all of us are born into sin. A closer look at this chapter reveals important insights into how this lack of obedience led to profound changes within Adam and Eve.

The first key point is that the enemy's strategy often involves twisting God's commands to make disobedience seem reasonable. In Genesis 3:1, the serpent asks, "Did God actually say, 'You shall not eat of any tree in the garden'?" Here, Satan's craftiness is evident; he takes an obvious command from God and encourages doubt. We see this tactic mirrored today when men ask, "Does the Bible really say we can't have sex before marriage?" This question is often the first step into deception, making God's boundaries seem restrictive rather than protective.

Satan knows our tendency to feel that God is withholding goodness from us, and he plays on that. Just as he knew how to exploit Adam and Eve's desires, he knows how to use our desires against us. Many men today perceive God's restrictions around sex as Him holding something good back, which is the same deception used in Eden. This has destructive effects, just as it did in Genesis.

Continuing to Genesis 3:2, Eve converses with the serpent: "We may eat of the fruit of the trees in the garden." The question arises: why was Eve even responding? We make room for sin when we entertain doubts and engage with deceptive ideas rather than standing firm on God's commands. It's like when people start rationalizing boundaries, saying, "It's only intercourse that's forbidden," while justifying other physical actions. But this reasoning is a trap—scientific research even shows that stimulating our bodies without the completion of intercourse can have negative effects on our mental and physical health.

Then, in Genesis 3:4, the serpent reassures Eve, "You will not surely die." We see the same tactic today as people convince themselves that they won't face consequences for their actions. The enemy's lies come in phrases like, "You won't get an STD" or "You won't lose your anointing." Satan only tells us what we want to hear because his goal is to rob God of His glory, particularly the glory He receives from our obedience.

Genesis 3:5 says, "For God knows that when you eat of it, your eyes will be opened, and you will be like God, knowing good and evil." While this verse isn't specifically about sex, it highlights a more profound truth about disobeying God's commands. Just as Adam and Eve's disobedience brought them a knowledge they were not meant to have, so does sex outside of marriage, which gives us an intimate knowledge of good (the pleasure of sex) mixed with evil (a knowledge of sexual intimacy without commitment). This knowledge binds us to a burden God never intended us to carry.

By verse 6, we see Eve convinced that the tree was "good for food" and "a delight to the eyes." She and Adam both eat, driven by the false promise that sin will satisfy. Every sin carries a lie that will fulfill a need we believe God is withholding from us. We convince ourselves that sex outside marriage is natural and beautiful, aligning with what culture tells us. But we are caught in the enemy's schemes when we fail to recognize the deception.

Finally, Genesis 3:7 tells us, "Then the eyes of both were opened, and they knew that they were naked." With this new awareness came shame. The Bible often reminds us that those who believe in God will not be put to shame, yet sin exposes us, making us feel ashamed. Think back to your first time having sex outside of marriage; that initial feeling of defeat and discouragement is common, especially for those of us who knew

God's command. I remember feeling that I had failed and that I had let down those who looked up to me as a man of God.

In shame, Adam and Eve sewed fig leaves together to cover themselves, initiating a cycle of secrecy mirrored in our lives. When we sin, we may try to hide it, yet God's covering, which keeps us from shame, is lost. God desires us to live with integrity so that if our lives were laid bare, there would be no secrets to shame us. Instead, He calls us to rely on His Spirit, empowered by His grace, to live according to His commands so we can stand before Him, unashamed and whole.

In many ways, sex is an act of faith in the promises that God has made. This spiritual reality is consistently depicted in the Bible, where fertility and infertility struggles are common, and God often performs miracles of conception. The Bible tells the stories of women who couldn't conceive and were heartbroken in a culture where bearing children was directly tied to the promise that a future rescuer would come through their family line. Even before this specific promise was given, conception symbolized God's faithfulness—a reminder that He sees, hears, and is near to His people.

For ancient Israel, the Bible shows a recurring pattern: Israel multiplied during times of oppression. This points to a deeper spiritual truth: the more God's people are oppressed, the more they grow. This reality remains true today, and it's a consistent theme throughout church history. Studies of Christian migration and evangelism show that faith has grown whenever persecution arises. Across cultures, a mysterious phenomenon occurs: when Christians face political, societal, or governmental oppression, the faith spreads rapidly, sometimes even consuming the populations that tried to contain it.

This has been true on every continent and is reflected in the revival currently happening in China. Although Christianity is outlawed there, it's experiencing explosive growth. Even in a nation where the government has placed restrictions on procreation, underground Christians are multiplying both in faith and in family. For Christians, procreation has always mirrored their spiritual presence. Holding a belief that no human authority can destroy, the faithful response is to raise children who carry the same conviction in their hearts.

As a testament to God's faithfulness in multiplying His people during persecution, sex is a spiritual act—a plea for God to continue His work through His witnesses on Earth. For couples facing the fears of infertility, every act of intimacy is a test of faith, a prayer for God's intervention to bless them with a child. Conception is a reminder that each new life is a miracle. Despite advanced technology designed to assist in fertilization, there's still no guarantee of pregnancy. This reinforces the truth that conception ultimately depends on God. Even as a supporter of science and grateful for these technologies, we must acknowledge that the power to create life is not ours but God's.

Sex, therefore, serves as humanity's reminder of the Creator. We don't control the creation of life—it happens in God's timing. While this doesn't mean that pregnancy only occurs in ideal circumstances and not in tragic ones like rape or abuse, it does mean that God remains sovereign, inviting us to recognize His power, authority, and presence over all human affairs. Those who reflect on sex and its outcomes often gain a deeper awareness of God. Even the exchange of chromosomes and genetic material during conception points to the fact that sex is not just a physical act but a profoundly spiritual one.

Sex—and particularly procreation—serves as one of the clearest representations of the natural order of God's kingdom.

Through the metaphors and parables Jesus used, we understand that the kingdom invades the world, creates new life, and grows to become the most dominant, noticeable presence among everything around it. Similarly, God's Spirit invades the flesh of a human, implants a living seed, and nurtures its growth until it consumes the whole person and spreads outward, impacting everyone they encounter. Eventually, this influence expands to entire communities, regions, nations, and, ultimately, the world. This is the powerful reality that sex reveals to us.

God's vision is for two people, aware of His sovereignty and purpose for sex, to come together intentionally, waging war on the kingdom of darkness by bringing kingdom children into the world. These children, raised in faith and with the wisdom of their family and elders, will grow up to impact everything around them for the kingdom of God. If we truly understood this spiritual aspect of sex, we would not be so quick to lie down with just anyone, recognizing the profound impact of the seeds we sow into an already fallen world. Too often, men fall prey to fleshly desires, resulting in children with a partner who may, at best, be indifferent to faith or, at worst, actively opposed to it. This lack of spiritual unity between parents can compromise the child's faith, just as God warned in Deuteronomy.

When one parent desires to raise the child as a citizen of God's kingdom, believing in Jesus and striving to expand His kingdom on earth, while the other parent undermines or outright opposes this mission, the child faces conflicting values. This lack of alignment can weaken the child's sense of authority, conviction, and power in their world. In such cases, a repentant man, aware of his past mistakes, often finds himself struggling to raise the child while also trying to minister to the child's mother, who may not share his faith. This situation was never God's intention for men. Ideally, men would lead their homes effectively toward

God, with a supportive spouse united in faith, allowing their children to thrive in the stability of parents who practice what they preach.

Satan's plan is exposed here: he often manages to create a situation that slows down a child's recognition of their purpose and calling. Yet, the beautiful and hopeful reality is that God, in His relentless pursuit of His children, remains faithful to use those He has called. Despite the mistakes and challenges, God often foils Satan's plans, redeeming the lives of those He loves. Many of you reading this may identify as children in such circumstances. Allow me to offer an illustration to clarify this idea further.

Tommy grew up in a loving Christian household with two dedicated parents who raised him and his siblings in church. From a young age, he developed a deep, personal faith. However, like many young adults, Tommy distanced himself from church life when he got to college, eager to explore the world outside his Christian upbringing. Though he maintained a relatively moral life, he met Jennifer, whom he perceived as a good Christian woman due to her strong moral character. They exchanged a verbal commitment to marry after graduation, and with this, they relaxed their purity boundaries and began having sex regularly.

In his final semester, Jennifer's unexpected pregnancy added pressure, but she managed to graduate before their child arrived. Tommy's family, however, disapproved of them having a child out of wedlock, so he and Jennifer quickly married and began setting up their home. As new graduates, they faced the challenge of finding stable careers to support their growing family. During this transition, Tommy noticed differences in how he and Jennifer wanted to raise their soon-to-arrive son. While Tommy emphasized the importance of prayer, Bible devotion, and church as central to their family life, Jennifer insisted that securing a full-time job was the priority before focusing on spiritual matters.

Tommy felt crushed by her resistance and regretted their premarital relationship, recalling his parents' warnings about saving sex for marriage to ensure alignment with family values. Despite the struggle, he remained a loyal husband, though he saw how their lack of unity affected their children, who became aware of spiritual truths but treated them as secondary. Recognizing this, Tommy bought this book on sexual purity and gave it to his sons for Christmas, hoping they would read it, find his story, see themselves, and make different choices to avoid repeating his mistakes.

When I consider sex as a spiritual activity, I'm confident in this belief because my wife and I have incorporated it into our prayer rhythms. Sometimes, we sense something is "off" in our marriage or feel the need to be extra intentional about aligning with one another on the things we bring before the Lord. For us, while regular Bible reading and prayer have always been foundational, sex has also become a way to recognize when we're misaligned and work toward realignment.

For example, during seasons when we're facing financial challenges or discerning God's will in difficult decisions, we don't just pray together—we intentionally "seal" those prayers with sex. This might look like having a specific spiritual goal or prayer request that we speak out loud to one another before engaging in intimacy. Not every sexual encounter involves this ritual, but when it does, it helps us align as a united front before God.

This practice is significant to us because we believe in the power of unity as described in the Bible. I've seen that certain seasons of our lives lacked blessings or answers to prayer due to a lack of unity. Realigning and being intentional together has often been the key to experiencing answered prayers and fully agreeing on what we're seeking from the Lord. We've even had supernatural experiences where we've prayed for healing—whether for ourselves or others—and decided to seal those prayers with sex. We've seen those prayers answered almost immediately on more than one occasion.

We believe these blessings are connected to our sexual union being within a covenant marriage, which honors God. This wouldn't have the same spiritual impact outside of marriage. Attempting this outside God's design would lack true unity and disrespect the Creator. For anyone reading this who is married and looking for deeper spiritual alignment with their spouse beyond prayer and Bible reading, I encourage you to consider sealing your prayers with sex.

Beyond this practice, we've also noticed that some of our most intimate and meaningful sexual moments often follow times of Bible study or prayer. Many times, these moments weren't planned, and we didn't intend to have sex afterward. However, sharing our hearts, praying, and connecting spiritually build a foundation for intimacy beyond physical attraction. In those moments, I'm most aware of my wife's deep love for Jesus and her devotion to Him and me. This stirs my desire for her in ways nothing else can.

Similarly, when my wife feels seen, heard, and loved—without any ulterior motives for sex—it often results in a beautiful moment between us. Women, unlike men, generally need emotional warmth and connection before intimacy. When my wife feels fully understood and appreciated, it opens the door to a meaningful experience where we're honoring the Lord with our bodies just as we did with our hearts.

I've heard it said that, like any addiction, sex is one of the most common because people often turn to it in their search for intimacy without realizing that their true longing is for intimacy with the Lord. This is why sex has the potential to be both incredibly powerful and extremely dangerous: for many, it becomes the very thing that prevents them from seeking the Lord and facing the truth of how deeply He desires their attention, worship, and affection. In the warmth of another's embrace, we can feel momentarily satisfied, blissful, even complete—yet numb ourselves to the deeper cry of our hearts for a love that transcends physical connection.

I know men who've been honest with me about their struggles with sexual addiction, whether it manifests physically with someone else or through pornography. They've shared that, in seasons where their focus strays from Jesus and the truth of the gospel, their addictions tend to flare up dramatically. These men recognize a spiritual reality far beyond sex: every human being was created to know God, as Romans 1 reminds us. According to this passage, when people turn away from God, they do so because they choose to suppress their innate knowledge of Him.

This speaks to what theologians call "general revelation" versus "special revelation." General revelation is the knowledge of God that all humans possess; it's evident in the world around us. Special revelation, however, reveals specifically who God is. People suppress their awareness of God by flooding their lives with activities and dopamine rushes that create a false sense of fulfillment. Such distractions make life more bearable, as discomfort often creeps in without them. Ironically, though, research shows that men who live this way—pursuing casual sex and a highly active sexual lifestyle—usually end up more depressed and aware of their inability to find lasting fulfillment.

In discussing the spiritual aspects of sex, I've heard it said before that orgasm is an earthly experience of heavenly bliss. Essentially, this person was attempting to communicate that the glory and heavenly feeling that is experienced during orgasm is synonymous with what every single eternal moment in heaven will feel like. While I had never thought of this on my own, I understand that this person was getting at the idea that sex points to a spiritual reality of heaven that we ultimately have to look forward to. This connection, I believe, is consistent with the idea that all great experiences on earth point to the reality that there is a supreme, eternal, and longstanding experience awaiting those who walk in obedience to God.

One of the spiritual realities Tim Keller explores in his book *The Meaning of Marriage* is that sex unites two individuals and transforms them into "one person". He says, "One Biblical author who is popularly thought to have a negative view of sex is St. Paul. Yet a closer look at what Paul actually says makes that hard to support. In 1 Corinthians 6:17ff, Paul forbids Christians from having sex with a prostitute. But the reasoning he gives is remarkable: Do you not know that a person who is united in intimacy with a prostitute is one body with her? For as it is said, "The two shall become one flesh.". . . Keep away from sexual immorality . . . for you do not belong to yourselves. You were bought with a price. Show forth God's glory, then, in how you live your bodily life. (1 Corinthians 6:17, 18, 20) What does this mean? Clearly "one flesh" means something different to Paul than mere sexual union, or Paul would be reciting a mere tautology: "Don't you know that when you have physical union with a prostitute you are having physical union with a prostitute?" Obviously, Paul also understands becoming "one flesh" here to mean becoming one person. One flesh refers to the personal union of a man and woman at all levels of their lives. Paul, then, is decrying the monstrosity of physical oneness without all the other kinds of oneness that every sex act should mirror."

One of the more profound mysteries of sex, and part of its spiritual dimension, is that it involves uniting and giving one's entire self to another. Spiritually, we understand that our journey with Jesus is an "all or nothing" commitment. Jesus made it clear to His disciples: to follow Him, they had to leave everything behind—including family, possessions, plans, and dreams. Similarly, the spiritual reality of sex mirrors this total surrender. When two people engage in sex, they're giving all of themselves, offering their whole being to the other person. This is why reserving sex for marriage is so essential; it's incredibly risky to give your entire self to someone who hasn't committed their life to you. Many people walk around, unable to truly know themselves, find their purpose, or understand who they are because they've already given themselves away. Often, they're not even in contact with the person who "owns" them now.

A profound spiritual insight here is that we have only one self to give. When we reserve sex for one person, we affirm that they're worthy of that commitment. As men, we often overlook this because women usually understand more deeply what it means to give oneself fully to someone else. Yet this truth applies to us as well.

This concept also explains the idea of renewed virginity. Only through Christ are we given the promise of being made new. Outside of Christ, we may have given ourselves away without knowing the spiritual consequences of premarital sex. But in Christ, we're born again, and our new self is something we can choose to give to another. This new self, tethered to God, has the privilege and responsibility of reflecting a pure surrender to God within a marital covenant, blessing those who witness it.

Sex, beyond this spiritual surrender, is also a sign of oneness. The massive success of the sex-help industry is a testament to the fact that a couple's sex life often reflects the health of their relationship. Counselors, sociologists, and psychologists have noted that when couples stop having sex, it can be a sign of a weakened bond. A natural desire to give oneself to the other is inevitable when unity, understanding, and sacrificial love flow between two married people. Authentic, healthy intimacy doesn't need to be forced; it's a natural outcome of connection and unity.

The Bible also communicates that sex unites two people in multiple aspects—emotionally, socially, economically, and even legally. This is why sexual relationships outside of the covenant of marriage lead to complications. When people engage in sex without the bond of marriage, they unknowingly introduce a level of incongruence that causes tension, jealousy, and feelings of entitlement. A man might feel he has the right to weigh in on a woman's decisions or lifestyle simply because they've been physically intimate. This sense of entitlement emerges because sex unites them in a way that makes each person deeply invested in the other.

Lastly, the Apostle Paul highlights a profound point about sex and marriage. He argued that it doesn't make sense to give your body to someone if you wouldn't also give your whole life to them. When he told men that their bodies belonged to their wives and vice versa, he underscored that sex and marriage involve a life fully submitted to the other. Yet, many today communicate this level of commitment casually, not realizing its spiritual and physical implications. This is one reason God's design for sex within marriage is wise and essential for human flourishing.

I believe a loving God has created a world with a God-sized void in every man's heart that only Jesus can fill. This is why, at the start of this book, I challenged readers to commit to abstinence until they finish reading. This challenge is, in part, a spiritual wager. I'm asking skeptics to test the truth of these claims rather than dismiss them outright. Any man genuinely seeking truth should be willing to face and evaluate it, free from distractions that cloud his perception of the realities within his soul and the world around him.

From my own experiences, I've seen that when men give themselves a season of isolation to hear God clearly, they often do. At that point, the question becomes whether they'll honestly respond to that call or continue suppressing the truth in rebellion. To every reader who's made it this far, I encourage you to keep going. You're already beginning a transformative journey by feeding your mind and spirit with these spiritual truths.

My prayer, and the prayer of the men who've shared their testimonies, stories, and research, is that those reading this book will encounter the gospel and sense the Spirit of God flowing through these pages. May you see that God desires a relationship with you and yearns for your undivided affection.

Reflecting on the themes we've journeyed through, it's clear that sex has always held a significance that goes far beyond the physical and emotional effects—it's deeply spiritual. Many ancient societies intertwined their sexual practices with their worship, convinced that sex could connect them to something transcendent. Though misguided, their actions reveal an important truth: that sex, by its very design, is meant to point us toward spiritual realities. Israel's story is a powerful testament to this. Surrounded by nations that used sex to honor their gods, Israel was commanded to follow a different path, a path that preserved the sacredness of sex. Yet, even they fell prey to idolatry and misuse of this gift, showing how easily we can misplace our affections and allow our desires to shift our focus from God.

This reveals a truth even more dangerous than we've discussed earlier. While we've seen that sexual choices can impact our emotional well-being, relationships, and life direction, it's the spiritual cost that should truly give us pause. Sexual sin doesn't merely compromise our personal lives—it hardens our hearts and distances us from God, the very source of life and purpose. Throughout scripture, sexual compromise is often depicted as leading directly to idolatry, a substitution of God's place in our hearts for something lesser. When we stray from God's design, we risk forming "soul ties" with those who do not share our faith, drawing us away from the truth we once held dear. This is why the Bible emphasizes that sex is sacred, meant to be an act of worship within marriage that reflects God's covenant love.

Each biblical warning against sexual sin builds toward this greater reality: our choices reflect our allegiance. Sexual purity, then, isn't merely a rule to be kept but a testament to where we pledge our hearts. The gradual insights we've uncovered should bring us to see that avoiding sexual sin is far more than protecting our physical and emotional well-being. It's about guarding our spiritual lives, maintaining our intimacy with God, and living in a way that honors His design. The stakes are higher than we may have realized at the start, and the call to purity is not about restriction but a profound, freeing alignment with a love that transcends anything this world could offer.

As we close this chapter, we reflect on the powerful truths shared above—truths that invite us to see sex as more than just an act of physical or emotional connection. At its deepest level, sex serves as a profound reminder of God's sovereignty, faithfulness, and creative power. The buildup of these insights has shown us that while emotional and physical consequences of premarital sex are significant, it is the spiritual implications that carry far greater weight.

Sex, as described, is a profoundly spiritual act, reminding us of our Creator's intentional design and His role in the miracle of life. Unlike other human experiences, procreation calls us to acknowledge that life ultimately stems from God. This sacred act was intended to happen within the bounds of marriage, not simply as a moral boundary but as a spiritual safeguard. Through marriage, two people come together in unity to reflect God's love, grace, and kingdom purpose. When we step outside of this covenant, we miss out on this divine alignment, and the powerful spiritual depth sex was intended to convey becomes obscured.

The stories of how God's people have multiplied under persecution and continued His work through challenges point us to the resilience and strength that faith can bring. Just as the faithful believers in China today, though oppressed, are growing and thriving spiritually, so too does God desire us to understand that even intimacy in marriage can be a profound statement of faith—a declaration of trust in God's plan. Every intimate act within a covenant marriage aligns us with God's greater story, contrasting sharply with the shallowness and potential despair that come from treating sex casually or with disregard for its deeper purpose.

This journey of understanding should serve as motivation to save sex for its rightful place within marriage. We are invited to see the spiritual danger of casual sex—how it can obscure the true purpose and beauty of intimacy designed by God. As we move into Chapter 7, we will explore how to live out this commitment to purity practically. We'll focus on intentional steps that lead to a life of honor, where abstinence becomes not just a rule but a path to experiencing God's deeper love and purpose.

CHAPTER 7:

The Challenge - Why and How to Practice Abstinence

For many, this chapter is the main reason why you picked up this book in the first place. Your desire to learn about abstinence was not solely a question about why it is important but more so for the equipping of yourself to be able to do this difficult thing. I know this is true because, in my experience, I've learned that many men are already convinced that abstinence is not only beneficial and is the way that God calls us to live but that they more particularly struggle with the practicalities of how to do it. I've also discovered that there are many men who, due to their habits and previous lifestyles of being sexually active, have cultivated rhythms of dating and engaging with women that are not conducive to the lifestyle that they hope to endeavor on. Many of these practices and cultural ways of engaging with women have become innate and even second nature, and the automatic aspect of these engagements often results in men being placed in compromising situations that war against their very desires for purity. With all this in mind, I am also excited to present this chapter to you as it contains critical pieces for men to grasp.

While many of these practices will serve you in your singleness and your encounters with women before marriage, many of these practices will still apply even after marriage for the man who is now tasked with remaining faithful and honoring to his spouse forever. I have been blessed to have many men lead me by example and share strategies with me that I have not only been able to incorporate but also experienced fruit from directly. Therefore, for many of the things that I will talk about in this chapter, I will provide my own experience alongside the concept and the ways that they have served me both in my time as a single and currently in my time as a married man.

My goal for this book is to prepare every man reading it to take the concepts we have talked about thus far and to actually live them out in a way that honors God, themselves, and the women we inhabit this earth with. I believe that through the practice of many of these disciplines and steps, men will find themselves more successful in their purity pursuits and that they will even be able to recognize the ways that they are better postured spiritually, emotionally, mentally, and even in their relationships with significant others and people in general. As we've already spoken, abstinence holds many benefits that extend well beyond the physical. As we embark on these practices, I want to encourage you as the reader who has committed to remain abstinent until the end of this book that you now—at the end of this chapter—will have the keys to be able to do precisely what you have set out to do. I am proud of every single person who has made it this far in this book, and I am honored to present to you the practices of how to live a life of sexual purity and abstinence.

Before I begin giving you this long list of practical strategies that will help you remain pure and abstinent, none of these in and of themselves are the recipe for being successful. While these tools will absolutely help you, these strategies must be accompanied by a deep heart change and a desire to please God. Otherwise, without the desire to please God—which is a greater motivation than anything we could conjure up on our own—and as a motivation that must come from Him, we are then best prepared and empowered to be able to live out a life of abstinence.

I must say this because many self-help books offer a bunch of strategies and solutions that ultimately leave men more depressed, miserable, and frustrated. This happens because they provide physical and strategic actions for men to take without ensuring they first have the spiritual empowerment to do such a task. While even the most disciplined man may be able to be abstinent for an extended period, only a man who has God's help will be able to maintain abstinence until marriage. Again, the goal of the person reading this book should be greater than mere self-improvement; it should be because they sincerely want to please God. Otherwise, any of your futile attempts to pursue abstinence will fall short and will be short-lived. On the most challenging days of my abstinent journey, I was reminded that God loves me, his commands are good, and that I had his Holy Spirit empowering me to make it through the difficult and tempting moments I found myself in. While there were days when this confidence was stronger than others, many of these strategies I will outline will help you in the moments when your faith is weak. But again, I must emphasize that these are not a list of strategies that in and of themselves will provide and guarantee success for a man who desires to live a pure life.

My biggest fear is for men to read this book, extract these strategies, and ultimately make them a law unto themselves, which has been the stain of purity culture in general. Purity culture has been notorious for amplifying the very sin problem that it set out to eliminate. This is because their solution for sin has been law instead of grace, which the Bible shows us is man's default way of handling a sin problem. When confronted with sin, we are often tempted to apply a law-based solution. Still, the Bible tells us in 1 Corinthians 15:56 that the "law is the strength of sin," meaning that wherever you make a law unto yourself, you are strengthening and empowering the very problem you have now tried to control. My hope is partly that you have picked up this book already experiencing and knowing the truth of what I am saying. I hope that you have picked up this book fully convinced that the practical strategies that I'm presenting—many of them not new to you—but that the difference between you attempting them before reading this book and after reading this book will be that you understand the spiritual component that unlocks the fruitfulness of these strategies.

I could never have remained abstinent without the Lord's help, and that is the testimony that I carry with me as the author of this book. It was nothing I did, and even the strategies I have—that I'll share with you—are unique strategies aligned with my convictions. That said, I invite you to read these forthcoming strategies, knowing that you have the freedom to incorporate whichever ones you feel the Lord desires for you to utilize. Not every strategy that I will speak about will work for every man, and not every strategy is God's will or desire for every man reading this book. Your struggles may not be mine because we are different and have different experiences. And the things and ways that I have specifically had to discipline myself may not be the same ways that you need to discipline yourself.

But with that being said, I have specifically chosen to implement the strategies and practices that are the most general and widespread among men. While the specific details and examples that I use—as they relate to me personally—may need to be tweaked, adapted, and changed to fit your personality and level of self-awareness, I invite you to pray about these strategies and see which ones the Lord has been saying to you. One hint that I'll provide you with is that if there is a strategy that you read that you feel like you've heard before or thought about before, it likely is one that you should incorporate. I've learned in my journey that revelation, specifically from the voice of God, is often confirmed. This means that if I share a strategy and it is not the first time that you've seen it or thought about it, then it is likely one that may be beneficial for you to implement into your life.

On the other hand, if there is one that you have never heard of before that seems incredibly extreme or unreasonable to you, I would challenge you to ask yourself why this seems absurd. It is in the challenges that I will present that seem the most irrational, where many of our areas of compromise can be exposed and, therefore, remedied. An example of this is that we also have to recognize that we live in a culture that is hyper-sexualized. Because of this, many of the strategies I will put forth in this book may seem traditional, archaic, or even like they will make us unattractive to the very relationships we hope and pray to be in one day.

I humbly invite you to trust me as I hope that our first six chapters of journeying together have given you comfort and exposure to my heart and desire for you as the reader. I have not included any of these practices and strategies as a way or means to manipulate or control you, but instead, I have included suggestions of things that you may try that have the potential to help set you free. I also invite you to experiment with some of these strategies and practices that you particularly disagree with and see how they work for you. One of the beautiful things about this journey is that our humility to learn from others means that we must be comfortable with change and trying things outside our comfort zone. Many of us as men have never known how to set healthy boundaries, so many of these strategies may be uncomfortable. Yet again, I invite you to apply a little bit of trust, not only in me but in the God Jesus Christ, who I believe has commissioned me to write this book.

Lastly, before we dive into the strategies ahead, I invite you to do something important. If this book has blessed, challenged, or encouraged you in any way, consider sharing it with other men who might benefit from it. With today's culture pushing hypersexualized messages on men, we need to provide truthful resources about the reality of sex and inspire men to embrace who God created them to be.

Please pass this book on to at least three men face-to-face, offering a personal recommendation to read it. Studies show people are more likely to engage with something recommended in person than online, though I fully encourage digital sharing as well. Together, we can help men pursue lives pleasing to God and committed to purity. Now, with no further adieu, let's move into some practical strategies for living a life of abstinence.

The most practical step I recommend for any man seeking to live a life of purity is to surround himself with people who hold him accountable and are committed to the same lifestyle. We naturally conform to the habits and goals of the people we spend the most time with, which is why accountability is crucial. As the saying goes, "You become like the three people you spend the most time with." Are those people pursuing goals that align with yours, or are they pulling you in a direction that compromises your purity? During my college years, accountability relationships with other men pursuing abstinence were essential for overcoming temptations. These men reminded me of my commitment to

God and helped me make different choices when others were leaving parties for sexual encounters.

One common mistake I've seen is men committing to purity without changing their friend groups. Hanging out with men who don't share the same values puts you in compromising situations and hinders your ability to stay mentally and physically pure. These accountability relationships are vital not only for avoiding sexual temptation but also for fostering open, honest communication. My friends would challenge me, asking tough questions about my interactions with women and holding me to a higher standard.

It's also essential to find accountability partners who don't struggle with the same issues as you. When men with the same struggles hold each other accountable, they often enable each other instead of challenging one another to grow. No man accomplishes any path toward purity alone. Just as addiction recovery programs emphasize the importance of accountability, pursuing purity requires surrounding yourself with people who strengthen your weaknesses and challenge you to be better.

Isolation, on the other hand, is a guaranteed path to compromise. In our society, which values independence, it's easy to believe we can handle things independently—but this mindset only leads to frustration. Real accountability isn't just about choosing people you like; it's about finding people who will help you grow, even if they aren't your first choice. It might mean submitting to the wisdom and guidance of someone older and more experienced, like a married man who can offer insights from his own journey.

In a time when many men resist submission, it's crucial to find someone you trust who can hold you accountable, someone who loves God and has your best interests at heart. This person must be able to disagree with you, challenge your decisions, and tell you "no" when necessary. Having a voice of reason outside your emotions will guide you through situations where attraction and emotions may cloud your judgment. Ultimately, this kind of accountability will help keep you grounded and ensure you make the right choices on your journey toward purity.

One of the critical things that helped me in my journey toward purity was avoiding isolation. In college, I lived in dorms where I always had roommates or accountability partners nearby, whether sharing the room or just down the hall. This meant I couldn't hide if I were doing something dishonest or sneaky. I learned the importance of accountability when I lived in downtown Atlanta, where I had a roommate who wasn't pursuing purity like I was.

Although I managed to avoid having sex, I would never recommend anyone follow my example of living with a roommate who didn't share the same convictions. During that time, it became much easier to compromise and put myself in difficult situations. I regularly witnessed my roommate bringing women into the apartment, letting them spend the night, and living a promiscuous lifestyle. Seeing this made me less strict with my decisions, leading to regretful situations.

In that environment, I even allowed certain women to spend the night, and while I pursued sex, God always intervened and protected me from going through with it. I felt like my roommate was having all the fun, and I struggled to understand why it seemed like he was still blessed, even though he wasn't living according to the values he claimed to hold. Being that close to sin weakened my resolve and tempted me to follow the same path.

Looking back, I believe that's why God shook up my life and moved me to New York, where He had a better living situation waiting for me. It was truly by God's grace that I didn't have sex during that season, but I still compromised in ways that harmed both myself and others. I gave in to inappropriate behavior like humping, touching, and tongue kissing—all consequences of living in a compromised environment without the support for sexual purity.

On top of that, I harmed the reputations of the women involved by lying to my roommate and telling him I was having sex with them when I wasn't. In doing so, I not only hurt those women but also damaged my Christian witness, making Jesus look bad in front of my roommate and the women I was compromising with.

This underscores the importance of surrounding ourselves with people committed to our well-being and aligned with our values. We need to live in environments that support our decisions and encourage us to live in a way that honors God.

Eventually, I found myself in one of the most ideal living situations: I moved into a discipleship house with several other Christian men, all committed to abstinence until marriage. Living in this house allowed us to share the same vision and life goals. We encouraged and strengthened one another well beyond regular visiting hours, giving us a deep synergy in Bible reading, prayer, and regular confession.

While this setup may only be realistic for some, it highlights the benefits of living in community. People who are surrounded by others with similar goals often flourish in ways that those in isolation do not. The intentionality within our household had such a strong impact on the men's lives. Every year, someone would get married and move out to live with their new wife. Another young, unmarried man would move in when this happened, and the cycle continued. We advertised the space as a place where men could share rent affordably while committing to surrendering to Jesus and holding each other accountable.

This house became a launching pad for men into healthy marriages, financial independence, and greater personal stability, and it was all rooted in the strength of our shared commitment to living godly lives in community.

Another practical way to avoid sexual temptation is by setting healthy boundaries. This strategy requires discernment and customization for each man, but the basic premise is the same. Boundaries are crucial because they benefit both sides, not just one person. When setting boundaries, it's important to remember that you protect yourself and the woman you're with. These boundaries should consider her needs as well as your own. This helps avoid creating extreme boundaries that might hinder the relationship or ignore basic things important to your partner. For instance, setting a boundary of no physical touch might be unrealistic, especially if your partner connects deeply through physical touch.

Establishing such a boundary could prevent you from even giving a friendly hug or holding hands, which could leave your partner feeling distant and disconnected. Instead, it's wiser to be specific about what kinds of touch are appropriate so you and your partner can still feel connected without triggering temptation. Part of setting healthy boundaries is ensuring both people involved understand and respect them. Open communication is vital—without it, boundaries are just ideas, not real guidelines. If your partner doesn't know your boundaries, she can't respect or help you stay accountable to them.

As men, we're called to lead by example. Initiating conversations about boundaries and intentionally setting them shows leadership and encourages your partner to reflect on her own boundaries. This strengthens the relationship and fosters a culture of commitment and exclusivity. In a world where dating is often seen as non-exclusive, clarity around boundaries is

 Why men shouldn't have sex before marriage

essential. I've spoken to several men who shared how dating has become more about exploring multiple partners than exclusivity, which shocked me because dating implied exclusivity in the time and place I grew up. This cultural shift reflects our hypersexual society and shows how boundaries are eroding.

When I was dating my wife, we had to set boundaries around space and time. For example, we agreed not to be in each other's apartments after a specific time and made sure people knew we were out together when we went on dates. These measures weren't just about accountability but also about maintaining healthy boundaries. I've even heard of couples who set boundaries around the time they ended phone calls, believing that late-night conversations increased their temptation to engage in inappropriate discussions or behaviors. While one person's boundaries might differ from yours, it's essential to recognize that boundaries are personal and should be tailored to your own struggles and self-awareness.

For example, I didn't need to set limits on phone call times with my wife because we were equally committed to purity. We didn't often drift into sexual conversations, and we were on the same page spiritually, which naturally removed some of the temptations other couples might face. However, that doesn't downplay the importance of communication—most couples still need to clarify their commitment to purity. Assuming that your partner automatically shares your values can be dangerous. In today's culture, even many Christians aren't clear that sex should be reserved for marriage. For 90% of people, a conversation about this commitment is essential.

Looking back, I see how I benefited from setting certain boundaries in previous relationships. When I was 16, I often had inappropriate conversations with the girl I was dating on late-night phone calls, and if I had understood the importance of boundaries, then I would have set them to prevent that. In my relationship with Denya, we didn't need those exact boundaries, but we still faced challenges.

At one point, due to our naivety and a lack of boundaries, my wife and I fell into bad habits of inappropriate touching that nearly derailed everything for us. Once these patterns start, they're hard to stop and usually escalate unless corrected. We realized we needed to set new, stricter boundaries to prevent ourselves from going down that path again. We decided not to be alone in each other's apartments and limited our indoor dates. This became so extreme that we started having our dates outdoors to avoid temptation.

Some may laugh at how extreme these measures were, but the fight for purity is serious. Satan doesn't play fair, and he wants couples to forfeit the blessings that come from doing things God's way. Giving up indoor dates was hard, especially as winter came, and we found ourselves freezing together on park benches, reflecting on the consequences of our lack of self-control. But this intentionality helped us reach the wedding altar without compromising our commitment to purity.

In the end, these boundaries, though challenging, were necessary to protect our relationship and our walk with God. The cold nights and the sacrifices we made were a constant reminder of the importance of honoring God in our relationship, and they ultimately helped us maintain our purity until marriage.

Through my conversations with many men, I've come to see the severe danger pornography poses in dating relationships striving for purity. Although the Lord had already freed me from pornography before I met Denya, many men have opened up to me about their ongoing struggles with it. They are ensnared by the cultural lie that pornography serves as a "healthy" substitute, supposedly keeping them from acting on their sexual desires with their partner. In reality, this lie not only keeps them in bondage but also works directly against the purity they're trying to maintain in their relationship.

Men consuming pornography convince themselves they're practicing self-discipline. But the truth is, they reinforce a lack of discipline every time they give in. While they may not physically engage in sex with their partner, they're conditioning their minds and bodies to give in to sexual desires whenever they arise. This will inevitably come back to haunt them in marriage when they realize their wife isn't an object created solely for their sexual gratification. The inability to deny their flesh now will make them more vulnerable to temptation later in marriage, creating difficulties both in their current relationship and in the future.

Men who watch pornography while pursuing abstinence with a partner are unknowingly corrupting the relationship. By consuming it, they're subconsciously training themselves to view women, including their partners, through a distorted lens, building a catalog of unrealistic sexual standards that will inevitably be projected onto their future spouse. As we've already discussed, this sets them up for sexual dissatisfaction because they'll compare their spouse to the various women they've encountered in pornography. Not only is this unfair to their future wives, but it also harms them and their relationships.

Pornography's addictive nature leaves many men chasing after a fantasy while neglecting the very real person right in front of them. In my mentorship with several men, I've seen how pornography continues to impact them even after marriage. Many turn to it as a coping mechanism, a direct consequence of failing to address the issue during their singleness. Some have even confided that they find themselves less attracted to their wives due to the virtual relationships they've built with countless women through pornography.

This underscores the need to fight for purity, not just from the physical act of sex, but from any form of pornography or explicit sexual content that compromises our hearts and minds. This battle is not just for the sake of purity now but to protect the health of future marriages.

One of the most effective strategies for overcoming sexual temptation is rooted in a principle often used in 12-step recovery programs like Alcoholics Anonymous: cognitive restructuring. These programs understand that much of the battle against addiction begins with changing how we think. For example, in the context of addiction, a person might replace the harmful thought, "I need alcohol to feel at peace," with the healthier belief, "I can find peace in other ways." This practice of reshaping our thoughts is just as crucial in our fight for sexual purity because it taps into one of the most vital keys to transformation.

Years ago, I learned a spiritual truth: if we remove something bad from our lives without replacing it with something good, that void will eventually be filled by something else negative. The replacement may not be the same thing we struggled with before, but because the void was left empty, it will likely warp into another harmful vice. A clear example of this came from a conversation with a friend who confessed that his ex-girlfriend had become an idol. He admitted that she controlled his happiness. Without her, he felt he had no reason to exist. He couldn't go 24 hours without checking her social media, and the emotional pull she had on him was damaging his mental health and sleep patterns.

As we talked, I asked about his past relationships to see if this was an isolated issue. He then revealed similar patterns with all his previous girlfriends. This was a breakthrough moment, as we both realized that the problem wasn't just his ex—it was the deeper void he was trying to fill through romantic relationships. Instead of addressing the root issue—seeking worth outside of God—he was replacing one woman with another. I shared with him that unless he replaced this unhealthy attachment with the one thing that could truly fill the void—God—he would continue to be oppressed by his relationships, or worse, he would find other things to idolize in his life.

This example highlights a crucial spiritual truth: it's not enough to remove negative habits or behaviors from our lives; we must actively replace them with what is right. For men striving to live a life of purity and abstinence, it's not enough to abstain from sex. You must ask yourself, "What will I replace it with?"

Based on my faith and experience with seeing men achieve victory, let me share the key: when you remove sex, pornography, and other destructive vices, you must replace them with intentional devotion to the loving God who created you. I challenge you to test this and experience the benefits for yourself. For those struggling with pornography, try replacing that time with prayer. But don't just stop at prayer—engage in the mental rewiring process. Speak out loud to yourself the truth that counters the lies you've been believing. Say, "Pornography is not what my body needs; my body needs intimacy with the Lord." Or, "Sex is not what will make me happy right now; intimacy with God will."

To experience the full power of this practice, take it a step further by speaking scripture aloud. The Bible reveals that scripture is our weapon against temptation. When Jesus himself was tempted, He quoted scripture as His defense. One man I interviewed, who has been married for many years, shared that quoting scripture amid temptation is his ongoing practice. He said, "Temptation is a normal part of life, and you must learn how to control yourself. Part of my control is if I see something that tempts me, I have scripture that I quote. "My body is for the Lord. The Lord is for my body." "I love my wife as Christ loves the church." I'm literally hitting that thing with the Word so I can make sure not to fall victim to it because it's very easy. And the other thing that can happen is social media, and if you don't have the right controls there or running into women in public who may try to shoot their shot because they see a man of God and they don't have anything to lose. I've gotta make sure I'm protecting myself in public places and also putting boundaries in place to protect against certain things. Temptation happens, but I don't fall prey to it 'cause I know the benefit of doing it God's way and doing something that adds value."

Much of our battles are internal, far removed from any physical actions that could get us into trouble. But this level of intentionality and discipline is necessary to live above reproach and avoid falling into sexual sin. Being overly vigilant is far more rewarding than relying on my own strength and assuming I can resist temptation. Overconfidence has been the downfall of many men, as scripture warns us not to even walk on the same side of the street as a woman we're attracted to.

In a practical sense, I go to war with my sexual temptations and desires in some extreme ways. As a married man committed to my wife, I make intentional decisions to avoid situations that could lead my heart astray. For example, I try to avoid getting on elevators or entering subway cars with attractive women. These are often spur-of-the-moment decisions, but they help keep my heart in check. If I see a woman in a train car—whether she's dressed provocatively or has a face that catches my eye—I intentionally choose another car. This helps me avoid lingering thoughts about another woman's beauty.

I don't prescribe this practice to every man, as it is a personal conviction between me and God. I encourage you to refrain from building a religious formula off my personal practices or those shared in this book. However, I strongly urge you to seek the Lord and establish your own practices for keeping your heart in check. Given the level of temptation in our hypersexualized world, such boundaries are often necessary.

Many men admit to struggling with wandering eyes and being tempted to lust after women in public. One man I interviewed shared his "ten-second rule." He explained, "If someone attractive is walking past you, count to ten slowly while walking away without looking back. Don't turn around. If the temptation persists, increase the number to twenty. Do whatever it takes to stay focused."

While some boundaries may apply differently to married men versus single men, the general principle remains: all men need boundaries to maintain sexual integrity. As a married man, one of my personal boundaries is that I refuse to be alone with a woman in a private setting. This includes car rides, houses, apartments, or any non-public location. Though this boundary has made life more challenging, it has also protected me in ways I am incredibly grateful for. I've seen many men fall because they lacked boundaries to safeguard themselves.

These boundaries help prevent the overconfidence that says, "I met with a woman I was attracted to, and nothing happened, so I can keep doing it." Instead, they lead us to say, "Even though I don't think anything will happen, I won't take the chance." When I was on staff at a church, this boundary meant I had to be very intentional about meetings with women. I ensured they were either on Zoom or in public places with witnesses. This not only protected me but also the women I met with. It's a boundary I highly recommend for any man in a position of influence.

Another practical strategy for maintaining sexual purity is to be mindful of what you expose yourself to. This includes external influences like media, films, music, and specific circumstances, situations, or locations. For instance, I know men who avoid massage parlors or nightclubs because of unwise decisions in their past. These places can trigger sexual responses, desires, and appetites that are unhealthy for them. For others, filtering the music, TV shows, and movies they consume is a key way to guard their hearts, minds, and bodies for purity.

As a musician, I was initially skeptical about the idea that music could influence our thoughts and tempt us sexually. For some reason, I failed to connect how it could affect our views on women and sex and lead us toward promiscuity. I've since learned that one way we can recognize that culture has influenced us is when we can't be convinced otherwise. In other words, if you're adamant that the music you listen to doesn't affect how you think about sex, that very belief is proof that it likely does. Interestingly, I never realized how much music hindered my purity until after I changed my music habits.

Here's how things unfolded for me: In late 2016, the Lord delivered me from pornography, but I still consumed all types of music. By 2020, during the height of the pandemic, I grew increasingly discontent with mainstream hip-hop and uninspired by it. This shift led me to spend more time listening to the gospel choirs and soundtracks I grew up with. Over the next few years, I listened exclusively to gospel music, and it was during this period that I noticed a significant change in how I viewed sex, women, and physical intimacy.

Switching to gospel music helped purify my mind and reduce the quick, sexualized thoughts I used to have throughout my day. My heart was less inclined toward perversion, and I also started muting social media accounts of women or people who posted content that made me stumble. This season of hyper-vigilance was part of the Lord's plan to purify and renew my heart. He completely transformed the way I thought.

After two years of only listening to gospel music, I began feeling a similar dissatisfaction with the mainstream gospel scene and started missing hip-hop. At the same time, I longed to rewatch some of my favorite hood movies, like Boyz n the Hood, Belly, and Paid in Full. After seeking prayer and wisdom from the Lord, I slowly reintroduced hip-hop music and mainstream TV and movies into my life. I had matured spiritually and developed a heart posture that allowed me to enjoy mainstream media without letting it control or shape my thoughts as it once did.

Today, I listen to all kinds of music and enjoy different forms of media, but I am hyper-aware of avoiding films with sexually explicit content. If the movie has a sexually explicit scene in it, I fast forward past the scene or close my eyes and ears like a little child. It's silly but important work. I do my best to avoid anything that contradicts my biblical beliefs or God-given convictions. I believe it's important for Christians to strike a balance—being engaged with culture without letting it undermine their foundation.

Again, this is an area where discernment and prayer are essential. What one man can listen to or watch without stumbling might be different for another. The goal is to be honest about our triggers and obedient to the Lord, knowing that to please Him, we must be willing to give up anything—no matter the cost.

In my opinion, one of the most effective ways to safeguard your sexual purity is through the spiritual discipline of fasting. Fasting is, unfortunately, one of the most underutilized practices among Christians today. I've noticed that many believers either don't understand its purpose or have misconceptions about its spiritual meaning, benefits, and objectives. This lack of understanding is why so many people have a negative relationship with fasting, and it's also why many fail to walk in spiritual power and authority.

Fasting is particularly relevant when dealing with fleshly desires and temptations because it involves bringing those cravings under submission to spiritual truth. In a traditional fast, your body craves food out of habit and routine. Yet, in fasting, you tell your body, "You do not control me. You are submitted to God, who dictates my actions and decisions." This act of self-denial not only reinforces spiritual discipline but directly combats the same bodily urges that also fuel sexual temptation. I've personally practiced fasting for over 20 years, starting in middle school, and have come to see how powerful it is in addressing physical and sexual desires.

While some people substitute traditional food fasts for things like social media fasts, there is something uniquely powerful about denying your body food. That's because the appetite for food and the appetite for sex are closely linked. Fasting doesn't eliminate your natural desires but forces them into submission to God's timing and design.

In my own life, fasting has been a crucial practice during times of heightened sexual temptation. Whenever I feel my sexual urges rising beyond control, I step into a fast. In those moments, I tell my body, "I will not feed you until you are fully submitted to the lordship of Jesus Christ and your appetite for fleshly gratification is broken." I don't set a specific end date for these fasts; instead, I fast until the sexual urges subside. Every time, without fail, as hunger intensifies, my body releases those cravings, and only then do I break the fast.

I first discovered this connection between food cravings and sexual desires during a fast, and it felt like a cheat code for life. Starving my flesh and feasting on God's Word realigned my mind with spiritual truths and deepened my dependence on God. Fasting forces me to live and think the way He wants, making me keenly aware of my need for Him.

For men seeking to preserve their sexual purity, I strongly recommend fasting during seasons of intense temptation. If you're struggling with pornography, masturbation, or premarital sex, fasting can be a game-changer. Fasting with a group of like-minded men can be even more powerful. My friends and I often fast together, reading the Bible and praying as a means of accountability. This has been transformative for us—both spiritually and physically. Frequent fasts not only help us reset from unhealthy eating habits, but they also give us dedicated time to intensify our prayer and Bible study.

I suggest a Daniel fast (fruits, veggies, and nuts) or a complete water fast for those embarking on a fast. Both will leave you hungry, creating opportunities for focused Bible reading and prayer. Many men who have contributed to this book, including myself, can testify to the power of fasting in bringing our fleshly desires under the authority of the spirit.

Finally, it's important to be aware of your most vulnerable seasons. Summer is incredibly challenging for me and many of my friends due to the prevalence of revealing clothing. During this time, I often fast weekly to keep my flesh in submission to the Spirit of God.

The final strategy for fighting sexual temptation may seem obvious to some, but it's about channeling your energy into other activities. Consider what makes good use of your time, helps you be productive, or promotes self-improvement. Given the physical and fleshly nature of sex, many choose to stay busy by going to the gym or engaging in sports. Others may dive into projects, explore the arts, spend time with friends, travel, or attend conferences. Directing your focus can be a powerful tool for those seeking to honor God with their bodies and hearts.

As we wrap up this chapter, I want to offer encouragement for those who might face ridicule from friends, family, or others for choosing a path of abstinence. I can't promise that every day will be easy, but I assure you the decision is worth it. On tough days, it's crucial to remember your "why." Surround yourself with people who support your choice and will help you stay focused when temptation or struggles arise. As I've said before, only those whose motivation stems from a love for God and a desire to please Him will ultimately succeed in this journey. Anyone relying solely on their own strength will find it difficult to endure. Embrace the process—even when it feels like you're missing out or Satan's lies grow louder—knowing that you're freeing yourself to become the best version of yourself and a healthier partner for your future spouse.

Use this season of abstinence to grow closer to God, learn about yourself, and focus on serving Him and positively impacting the world. It's always easier to stick with a challenging task when you're motivated and reminded of why you started in the first place.

I also want to give hope to those who are not abstinent and are sexually active. Some of you may feel regret or wish you had found this book sooner. But it's important to understand that there is always time to make a life change. If you're encountering these truths now, then now is the appointed time for you to live by them. God, in His kindness, has given you this resource to help you live better for yourself and the generations that come

 Why men shouldn't have sex before marriage

after you. You have the chance to be an example to others who are searching for direction. You are not defined by your mistakes or your past. Today is a new day, and remember that the Lord is with you, empowering you with His Spirit as long as you choose to trust and believe in Him.

Before moving forward, I encourage you to take a few important steps. First, seek forgiveness from God and then forgive yourself. It's hard to walk a new path while carrying guilt. Since God has freed you from that guilt, receiving His forgiveness and extending that same grace to yourself is essential. This will help you move forward with confidence and authority.

Next, recommit yourself to purity. Make a commitment not only to yourself but also to someone you trust. This creates accountability and ensures that your commitment is solid.

Lastly, lean into the testimonies shared throughout this book from men who have turned their lives around after being sexually active. Their stories offer wisdom and insight, proving that change is possible and reminding you that you're not alone in this decision. Focus on Christ, His grace, and the renewal that comes through His Spirit. Let the past stay in the past, and walk confidently in front of a world that's watching.

CHAPTER 8:

The Bigger Picture:
Why Your Choices Matter

Many people, particularly in college, adopt the mindset that this is their chance to have sex freely and frequently. I remember a friend once told me, "This is my chance to have sex as much as I want. This is what college is all about." On the one hand, I knew what he meant—college often feels like a time of freedom, with minimal oversight or long-term consequences. But on the other hand, I knew he was terribly mistaken. While many of my peers would go on to engage in sexual relationships throughout their college years, I could already see how this would haunt them long after they graduated. They would wrestle with the emotional baggage, guilt, and complicated relationships they had accumulated during that time. The evidence was all around me, even in the church—pastors and leaders losing their jobs and families due to affairs and sexual misconduct. The more I observed, the clearer it became: sex has the potential to be both incredibly beautiful and profoundly damaging when misused.

We are constantly bombarded by the consequences of sex outside of marriage. Turn on the news, and you'll see stories of sexual exploitation, infidelity, and assault. These stories are no longer limited to college campuses or consensual relationships. Day after day, we are confronted with tragic accounts of rape, child molestation, and sexual violence. What's even more heartbreaking is that many of the perpetrators were once victims themselves, trapped in a cycle of abuse. Science backs this up—those who experience sexual trauma outside of a loving, committed relationship are often the ones who struggle to cope and, tragically, pass that harm onto others. While this is a broad generalization, the pattern is undeniable: sex outside of a healthy covenant relationship often leads to pain, confusion, and brokenness.

On the other hand, those who choose to reserve sex for marriage tend to experience a different outcome. These individuals are more likely to preserve their jobs, maintain healthy relationships with their families, and experience inner peace. They avoid creating victims of others and uphold a sense of integrity in their personal and professional lives. So how can we, as a society, claim to be committed to creating a better world—one free from sexual violence and abuse—without acknowledging the role that returning to traditional sexual values plays in that mission? The most effective step we can take toward healing the deep wounds caused by sexual immorality is to recognize the value of reserving sex for marriage.

As I debated with a friend, we found ourselves locked in a disagreement about sex. I argued that waiting for marriage guaranteed the best sex of my life, while he claimed the opposite—that exploring multiple partners would give him a better understanding of what he desired. For him, learning about his body and preferences through various encounters would supposedly ensure that he wouldn't settle for less in the long run. But for me, the motivation to wait was deeper. After ten years of celibacy, I understood the value of fully renewing my mind and preparing myself to appreciate my future wife. I wanted to avoid comparing her to anyone else. Even more importantly, my decision wasn't just about agreeing with God's law but was rooted in a deep love for Him. Whether or not I agreed with every rule, my faith in God's goodness guided me, knowing that His way would ultimately lead to the most fulfilling outcome. On the other hand, my friend lived according to his philosophy, embracing hook-up culture and non-commitment. He was upfront with women about his intentions, which worked in his favor, ensuring that his desires for access to their bodies were met.

Ironically, despite his casual approach to sex, my friend longed for marriage, just as I did. He wanted a deep relationship where he could be known, loved unconditionally, and supported by a partner who would help him grow and achieve his goals. Yet, his view of sex as part of the trial period of getting to know someone was exactly what kept him from forming the relationships he so desperately desired. Most of the women who were willing to give him access to their bodies without commitment didn't want to commit to one man either. They shared his view of relationships, and when their bonds inevitably failed, both sides seemed surprised by the instability. It was a puzzling cycle—how could one seek stability while building a foundation on unstable ground?

There are countless reasons why premarital sex harms us now and destroys our future prospects. As I advocate for a return to traditional values, it's important to recognize that what some call "old school" didn't face the "new school" problems we face today. While the world has never been entirely free from sexual abuse, history shows us a time when those numbers were drastically lower because sexual relationships were primarily confined to marriage. If we step back and reflect on what we truly desire for ourselves and society, the contradiction becomes clear. We want happiness, security, and love, and we want a world where our neighbors are safe from abuse, manipulation, and exploitation. Yet, if we reject the idea of reserving sex for marriage, we are, in essence, hypocrites. It is impossible to want a better world while simultaneously demanding the freedom to engage in sex whenever and with whomever we choose.

By waiting until marriage, we avoid many obstacles that often arise in relationships. Every decision we make carries consequences, whether or not we're thinking about them in the moment. Too often, people focus on the present, enjoying the moment without considering how today's choices will follow them into their marriages and relationships. But sex always has consequences, both immediate and long-term. We deceive ourselves when we think we can escape those consequences, and this belief reflects our misunderstanding of God's sovereignty and justice. We cannot choose our consequences; they will always catch up with us.

There are physical consequences to sex, and people tend to focus more on these. But we often overlook the emotional aspect of sex. Many deny that men experience emotional residue from sexual encounters, but this simply isn't true. While my own experiences are limited, having chosen celibacy outside of marriage, I've spoken with many men who have had different experiences. Through these conversations, I've realized that men often downplay the emotional weight of sex. This may be because society doesn't teach men to be in tune with their emotions. Many men struggle to articulate how they feel at all. Experts even suggest that most men can't give a clear answer when asked about their feelings. We are not pushed to develop emotional intelligence or health, which contributes to our inability to grasp the emotional consequences of sex fully. But just as men can learn to shut off their emotions, women can as well, creating a dynamic where neither party fully engages with the emotional side of intimacy.

When we reduce sex to a purely physical act, stripping it of its emotional and spiritual components, we lose sight of its true power. Sex is meant to be the deepest form of connection between two people, as close as two individuals can become. Reducing it to a mere physical encounter is a reflection of how far we've drifted from understanding the sacredness of sex. This disconnection often stems from trauma—people shutting off their emotions to protect themselves from the vulnerability that comes with intimacy. It's a coping mechanism, allowing someone to experience physical closeness while keeping their heart closed off, unwilling to be fully known or loved.

Several men I've interviewed expressed that they only recognized the guilt, shame, and regret associated with their sexual past after becoming born-again Christians. Their transformation allowed them to see the emotional and spiritual costs of their previous lifestyles, and they began to understand that sex outside of marriage was not just about physical pleasure but a deeper disconnection from God's purpose for their lives.

Being intentional in relationships is about transparency, even when it makes you vulnerable. When a man expresses his desire to pursue abstinence and honor the Lord through that decision, he opens himself up, hoping that the woman will respect and share his convictions. However, there is always the fear of rejection—will she still want him despite his choice? Will she honor his commitment, or will his intentionality turn her off? After laying his heart bare, a man wants to know that the

 Why men shouldn't have sex before marriage

woman he's pursuing will stand beside him in that decision. The real challenge arises when men convince themselves they can maintain a healthy relationship with a woman who doesn't share the same commitment to abstinence. If she doesn't embrace that discipline herself, his conviction alone won't be enough to carry both of them.

This often creates a battle of wills, where she may unintentionally (or even consciously) try to weaken his resolve while he tries to convince her to adopt a lifestyle she isn't committed to. This dynamic is dangerous and breeds temptation. Unfortunately, some men and women even see this as an enticing challenge, enjoying the thrill of trying to influence the other, leaving the door open for sex despite their stated intentions.

Men, no matter how old they are, who are serious about pursuing purity and abstinence need accountability. I've been amazed by how some men enter dating relationships, stumble along the way, pulling their partner closer to God while constantly fighting to maintain boundaries, and then expect marriage to transform everything magically. If they couldn't hold each other accountable and spiritually uplift one another before marriage, why would that change after the vows?

The compromises we make at the beginning of a relationship often become the very frustrations we carry into marriage. Ignoring these early warning signs only sets us up for disappointment later. Abstinence before marriage isn't just a physical decision but one that strengthens emotional and spiritual resilience, paving the way for a stronger marriage built on shared convictions.

Many women I've spoken with don't believe abstinent men are common. They think finding a man serious about purity is nearly impossible. In reality, part of the motivation for writing this book stems from the fact that there are abstinent men—but many of them, like myself, hide their commitment to purity. In a world that often mocks or dismisses this decision, we've been more afraid of what culture thinks than of honoring God. As a result, we've been silent, allowing the world to believe that men like us don't exist.

This silence has created a sad phenomenon: many men wait to share their testimony of purity after they've already crossed the finish line into marriage, robbing the single men and women around them of the encouragement they need. If more men were open about their commitment to abstinence while they were still walking that path, it would create a ripple effect of boldness, strengthening others to follow in their steps. The world needs to see men living for Christ and honoring Him in their purity, not hiding their devotion until it's too late to inspire others.

Today's culture—fueled by porn, social media, and the normalization of hook-up culture—makes sexual temptation much more accessible than it was for previous generations. With sex increasingly trivialized and treated as a casual commodity, men must be even more intentional about setting boundaries. Purity in this fast-paced, instant-gratification world requires a stronger commitment than ever.

Marriage is a commitment to love all aspects of a person—the good, the bad, and the ugly. In order to love someone fully, you must see them fully, including their weaknesses, flaws, and past. That's why it means so much when someone says "I love you" after seeing the real you. It assures you that even the unlovable parts of you are accepted.

Yet, we live in a time when people are less willing to have honest conversations about their sexual past, body count, or history. Avoiding deep, meaningful conversations leads to shallow relationships, where true love—love that accepts every

 Why men shouldn't have sex before marriage

part of the person—cannot thrive. Real love, the kind that creates a lasting marriage, demands vulnerability and honesty. Without it, relationships will continue to miss the essential ingredient that allows them to grow: a genuine, unconditional love that mirrors Christ's love for us.

Sex has a profound connection to our spiritual life, whether we realize it or not. For those who aren't Christians or are still exploring the reality of God, engaging in sex outside of His design can create a spiritual barrier that makes it harder to hear His voice. While it's not impossible to encounter God while living a sexually active lifestyle, it often serves as a distraction from fully experiencing Him. This is because sex is both a physical and spiritual act. God designed humans as whole beings—mind, body, and spirit. What we do physically impacts our relationship with Him spiritually. The Bible makes this clear: If we love God, we will bear the fruit of that love in our actions. If we love Him, we will love our neighbor, live righteously, and make choices that reflect His will for our lives. Yet, many live as though their sexual decisions and relationship with God are separate. I meet men who express frustration about their unanswered prayers or say they've "tried God," only to realize that their attempts were conditional. They were trying God while continuing to live their own way, not surrendering to His guidance.

This selective approach to God prevents many from truly experiencing His presence. We cannot fully "try" God if we are still the God of our own lives, doing what we want without submitting to Him. Surrendering their bodies to Him can be the first step for those unsure of where to start in their relationship with God. Abstaining from sex may be the very decision that opens the door to a transformative encounter with God. Though there's no guarantee of a specific spiritual experience, it's worth taking the chance to discover if living life His way leads to deeper fulfillment.

This isn't about advocating a works-based theology but rather about understanding that what we do with our bodies has real spiritual consequences. Imagine if I bought you healthy groceries free of charge, but instead, you insisted on spending your own money on junk food. The groceries would benefit your health, but you'd miss out because you prefer what you're used to—even though it may harm you. In the same way, many people are clinging to sex, believing it's the best thing for them, when in fact, they're forfeiting something better—God's presence and His best for their lives. What if you found out that intimacy with God is more fulfilling than sex, but you never know because you're holding onto what you think you need? This is the reality for many today. They are trading God's best for a temporary pleasure that leaves them spiritually malnourished.

To fully understand the weight of this, we must turn to the Bible, specifically the account of the first sin in Genesis 3. When Adam and Eve disobeyed God's command, they set in motion the consequences of sin that continue to affect us today. One of the most cunning tactics of Satan was to make Eve question what God had explicitly said. In Genesis 3:1, the serpent asks, "Did God really say, 'You must not eat from any tree in the garden'?" This same tactic is still at work today, especially when it comes to sexual sin. Many men ask, "Does the Bible really say we can't have sex before marriage?" This question reveals a similar deception—that God's boundaries are somehow withholding His goodness from us. Satan's lie is that God's commands limit our happiness, when in reality, they protect us and lead us to true joy.

Eve's mistake wasn't just in doubting God's word but in conversing with the enemy. Genesis 3:2 shows her responding to the serpent, "We may eat from the trees in the garden…"—

instead of standing firm in what God had told her. This mirrors our rationalizations today: "It's just foreplay." "Oral sex isn't really intercourse." "As long as we don't go all the way, it's fine." But by entertaining these thoughts, we are already stepping into the trap that leads to spiritual death. Research even shows that sexual stimulation without release can harm both our minds and bodies. But more importantly, these compromises erode our spiritual integrity.

Satan's next move in Genesis 3:4 is to directly contradict God, telling Eve, "You will not surely die." We fall for similar lies today:

- "You won't get an STD."
- "You won't get her pregnant."
- "You won't become emotionally attached."

The enemy whispers what we want to hear, playing on our fears and desires. But the truth is, Satan doesn't care about our well-being—he only seeks to rob God of His glory, particularly the glory that comes from our obedience. By honoring God with our bodies, we reclaim the fullness of life He intended for us.

Genesis 3:5 holds a profound truth that sheds light on why men shouldn't have sex before marriage. The verse reads, "For God knows that when you eat of it, your eyes will be opened, and you will be like God, knowing good and evil." While this verse speaks of Adam and Eve's disobedience in eating the forbidden fruit, I believe the underlying principle applies to sex outside of marriage as well. The knowledge we gain from disobedience, especially in matters of sex, is not what God intended for us. The enemy manipulates our limited understanding, convincing us that the forbidden knowledge of good and evil is desirable when, in fact, it brings harm and distance from God.

Before Adam and Eve sinned, they only knew good—what God had shown them. They were intimately acquainted with it. However, disobedience brought them into an intimate relationship with evil as well, something God never intended. This intimacy with both good and evil parallels what happens when we engage in premarital sex. We come to know, experience, and bond with the beauty of sex, something good that God created, but we also become intimately bound to the evil that comes from using it outside of God's design.

The Hebrew word "yada" used in Genesis 3 for "knowing" is the same word used in Genesis 4 to describe Adam's sexual intimacy with his wife. This suggests that Adam and Eve's disobedience introduced them to the knowledge of both good and evil in a deeply personal, experiential way, just as premarital sex introduces us to a dual knowledge of both the good that sex offers and the evil of misusing it. When we step outside of God's boundaries, we bind ourselves to this intimate knowledge of something that can corrupt our view of sex. This is why so many who engage in sex outside of marriage struggle with sexual sins later—they unknowingly become attached to the wrong kind of knowledge, just as Adam and Eve's eyes were opened to the wrong knowledge after they ate the fruit.

Verse 6 of Genesis 3 further explains the nature of sin. It tells us that the woman was convinced: "So when the woman saw that the tree was good for food and that it was a delight to the eyes, and that the tree was to be desired to make one wise, she took of its fruit and ate, and she also gave some to her husband who was with her, and he ate." Here, we see two key elements in sin: a false promise and deception. Eve believed the forbidden fruit would bring wisdom and fulfill a need that God was withholding from her. In the same way, many people today are deceived into thinking that sex outside of marriage will provide fulfillment and beauty when, in fact, it leads to brokenness and shame.

Genesis 3:7 is a pivotal verse highlighting the consequences of disobedience: "Then the eyes of both were opened, and they knew that they were naked. And they sewed fig leaves together and made themselves loincloths." Immediately after their disobedience, Adam and Eve felt shame. This shame was new—they hadn't known they were naked before. Similarly, when we engage in premarital sex, we gain a knowledge we weren't supposed to have, a knowledge that brings shame. This shame results from entering into something God designed for marriage but using it in a way that falls short of His will.

For those of us who have already had sex outside of marriage, we can likely recall a moment of shame after the act. I remember feeling defeated after my first time, not just failing myself but also feeling like I had failed the woman I was with—someone who needed to see a man of God living a life of integrity. This cycle of shame often starts with the realization of our nakedness—our exposure—and the loss of God's covering. We see this with Adam and Eve when they attempt to cover themselves with fig leaves. Before their disobedience, they didn't need to cover their nakedness because God's covering was sufficient. In the same way, God's grace and covering protect us from shame, but when we step outside of His will, we expose ourselves to it.

This shame reminds us of our need for Jesus. Scripture repeatedly tells us, "Everyone who believes in him will not be put to shame." Jesus is all we need to be fully satisfied in life, including our sexual desires. However, when we enter into a sexual relationship outside of marriage, the intimacy with sin causes us to feel that shame.

One thing that kept me in the struggle with pornography for so long was the lie that I was preparing myself for sex by watching it. I believed that if I wasn't having sex, porn was a way to know what to do when the time came. But the truth is, sex is about learning each other. When you go into a relationship believing you should already know everything, it robs you of the journey that God intended for marriage—the journey of learning each other's bodies together. This shared vulnerability and discovery are what make sex beautiful and strengthen the bond between spouses.

On the other hand, even abstinence doesn't guarantee a great sex life in marriage. It's important to understand that waiting doesn't automatically result in perfection. However, saving sex for marriage allows you to experience it without comparison. It becomes the best sex you've ever had because it's the only sex you've ever known. This can be a powerful reason why sex within marriage is more fulfilling—it's untainted by the world's false standards.

We aren't doomed if we didn't do things God's way, but doing it His way gives us a glimpse of His heart. God's desire is not for us to find satisfaction solely in our sex lives but to protect us from the weight of comparison and the damage that sin brings. Porn, for example, conditions us to believe that sex should always be 100%, no misses, and constantly exciting. But this is a lie that leads to disappointment and frustration in the real world. It's a trap that sets unrealistic expectations for something that was never meant to be perfect in the way the world portrays it.

Marriage offers an ongoing journey, not a one-night stand. With every sexual encounter, there is an opportunity for growth, improvement, and feedback. The pressure to perform perfectly fades when both partners are committed to learning and showing up better each time. In the safety of a healthy marriage, where the mindset is "I'm not leaving, I'm committed to you," the focus shifts from perfection to service. Great sex isn't measured by flawlessness but by sacrifice, thoughtfulness, and a willingness to prioritize the other person. This mindset fosters deeper intimacy and ever-improving connection.

Yet, even with God's desire for us to experience satisfaction in our marriages—both in our sex lives and overall health—we must remember that we live in a fallen world. Sometimes, our reality does not align with our hopes. What happens when you've honored God with your purity and realize that the sex life you imagined may never be fully realized?

Men, in particular, are often burdened with societal expectations to perform like professionals in the bedroom. On my first wedding night, I was nervous, conditioned by a culture that told me, "If you don't impress her tonight, she's gone." That pressure only led to stress, and as many men know, stress and nerves hinder sexual performance. I had to mentally work through these anxieties, reminding myself that our marriage wasn't built on this one moment but on a lifelong commitment. It was freeing to realize that I didn't have to be perfect right away. She had already committed her life to me, and I to her. Over time, I learned to relax, grow, and embrace the learning process, which made our sexual relationship stronger.

When men don't feel emotionally safe, when they're consumed by performance anxiety, it can prevent even basic physical arousal, like achieving a full erection. Safety in a marriage isn't just emotional—it has tangible effects on sexual performance and fulfillment.

Tim Keller's The Meaning of Marriage discusses how differing sex drives between partners can create challenges, but the focus in marriage should always be on serving and pleasing your spouse, even when you might not feel like it. This sacrificial love is the cornerstone of a healthy and thriving sexual relationship.

It's common to enter marriage with the belief that sex will happen every day, only to be met with the realities of life. Fatigue, responsibilities, and other factors often challenge that expectation. Conversations about sex and abstinence are crucial, not only for preparing ourselves but for guiding the next generation. However, we must also acknowledge a critical truth: God doesn't owe us anything. This is where purity culture has failed many of us by fostering the belief that if we keep ourselves pure, God is obligated to bless us with a perfect marriage or sex life.

While God doesn't owe us anything, we are still called to be faithful and responsible. If we don't prepare well for the blessings He may want to give us, it's as if we're telling Him, "You can't trust me." Our abstinence shouldn't be a transaction, a way to force God's hand. Instead, we remain abstinent because we love God and trust Him. In doing so, we are also preparing ourselves for the possibility of experiencing the best sex ever within marriage and for the deep, long-lasting satisfaction that comes from obeying His word.

One of the primary reasons abstinence is so important is the potential for long-term legal and financial consequences when responsibility in this area is neglected. We haven't yet discussed the emotional and financial toll of child support and custody disputes, but now seems like the right time to address it. In my adult life, as I've mentored men and been married to a woman raised by divorced parents, I've witnessed firsthand the emotional impact of custody disputes. This experience has only strengthened my conviction that a lack of planning, commitment, and preservation of sex until the right time has left countless families in situations where their children end up as "property" to be divided by the courts.

It breaks my heart to see so many children removed from stable homes and thrust into lives marked by deep insecurity. As

 Why men shouldn't have sex before marriage

a father, I now clearly see the beauty and strength that stability provides. Parenting is the most demanding job I've ever taken on. Yet, the rewards are unmistakable—especially when I see the difference stability makes in my children's lives compared to those who don't have it. Adolescence is already a confusing time of self-discovery, filled with new environments and challenges. However, when children also face the insecurity of shifting between their parents and homes, it adds a level of difficulty that no child should have to bear.

One of the unique struggles for children in these situations is having to adapt themselves based on which parent they're with. This constant need to change identities depending on the environment creates a habit of compartmentalization that can stifle their growth. It often pushes children to develop skills in manipulation, learning how to "perform" for certain situations rather than authentically being themselves. While adaptability is a necessary life skill, children need the security of both their mother and father as they navigate who they are in a vast world.

Custody arrangements frequently create extremes: one parent's time with the child is centered around school and activities, while the other's is based on vacations and fun. This imbalance prevents children from experiencing a holistic, balanced relationship with each parent. For example, a young boy who only sees his dad during weekends or vacations misses out on the structure and responsibility that might come from a father's presence during the week. On the flip side, because the father sees this time as precious, he may feel guilty about enforcing discipline, leading to a relationship that's all rewards and no responsibility. This dynamic can be harmful because discipline is essential in building a loving and respectful parent-child relationship.

Similarly, a child who spends all school days with his mother might only see her in the context of schedules, chores, and responsibilities, missing out on the lighter, more relaxed side of her personality. Intentional co-parenting can alleviate some of these issues, but living separately inevitably brings a level of disconnection. Even when parents work together, children learn how to "work the system" for their benefit, putting them in control of relationships that should be led by their parents. This lack of alignment between parents under separate roofs creates gaps in communication and consistency, leaving children to navigate complex dynamics on their own.

I want to be clear: I'm not suggesting that two-parent households are always the ideal solution or better than single-parent homes. There are countless cases where a single mom or dad is the better option for raising a child, and I honor the incredible sacrifice and hard work that single parents make every day. In my own marriage, I've learned that an ununified home with two parents can be more harmful than a single-parent household where balance and consistency are present. While having both parents in the home isn't the ultimate solution, being on the same page and working together is critical.

Returning to my main point, premarital sex often complicates families in ways that parents never anticipate, with unplanned pregnancies or weak commitments having lasting effects on children. Let's look at the story of Marcus, a man who wanted to be a devoted father to his son, Jalen, but who struggled under the consequences of an early decision. When he and his then-girlfriend Brianna first met, he wasn't looking for a serious relationship, but things escalated quickly, and before long, Brianna was pregnant. Though they tried to stay together for Jalen's sake, their relationship soon fell apart. Brianna moved on, dating a string of new men, some of whom she introduced to

Jalen early. Her lifestyle was unpredictable—she changed jobs often, and her fluctuating income forced them to relocate every few months. Each time Brianna moved, Marcus faced another battle to find where his son was, keep up with Jalen's schedule, and somehow maintain his own commitments.

But it wasn't just the constant upheaval that made things difficult for Marcus. Brianna's mother, who wasn't fond of him from the beginning, grew into a vocal critic. Brianna would vent to her mother about him whenever they argued, further straining an already difficult situation. As a result, Brianna's mom became deeply involved in the custody process, pushing back on any attempts Marcus made to have consistent time with Jalen. When Brianna was frustrated, her mother became her support, complicating things further by constantly questioning Marcus's role and reliability as a father. Despite Marcus's efforts, he couldn't shake the negative image they'd painted of him, no matter how much he showed up for his son.

When they went to court, Marcus was granted weekends with Jalen, but that didn't go as smoothly as he'd hoped. Though he had the court's permission, there were countless times Brianna and her family would push back. Sometimes they'd call last-minute, claiming Jalen was sick, or they'd make alternate plans without consulting him. Each time Marcus tried to address it, he faced resistance, creating a tense environment every time he picked Jalen up. As much as he wanted to fight for more time in court, he was exhausted and financially drained from previous legal battles. With each disappointment, Marcus felt the weight of his frustration and his son's growing distance.

One of the hardest parts for Marcus was knowing that his son was watching it all. Jalen began to ask him questions that no child should have to consider, like why he didn't live with him or why his mom and grandma spoke poorly about him. Marcus, not wanting to add to Jalen's confusion or hurt, tried to shield his son from the complex emotions he felt. But as Jalen grew, he noticed his son becoming more withdrawn and reserved. He saw in Jalen the same need to "fit in" with his mom's boyfriends, to adapt to each new environment, and to adjust his behavior to keep everyone happy.

Looking back, Marcus often thought about how different things could have been if he had waited to bring a child into the world under more stable circumstances. He wanted to give his son the security of a united home, but instead, he had to witness Jalen's struggle to understand where he fits in a fractured family. He realized, painfully, that the choices he made before Jalen was even born were affecting his son's future, forcing him to navigate adult insecurities far too young.

For men reading this, Marcus's story is a stark reminder that sexual responsibility isn't just about the present. The choices you make today can shape the lives of your future children in ways you might not foresee. It can mean the difference between giving them the stability they deserve or leaving them to pick up the pieces.

Few people recognize just how challenging child support can be for men, particularly since statistics show that men are rarely awarded custody of their children. This disparity has deep roots, with court battles dating back to the 1970s when unwed fathers first demanded equal treatment under family law. At the time, the law required unwed fathers to meet extra legal conditions to gain custody rights—conditions not typically required of unwed mothers. Even today, custody decisions overwhelmingly favor the mother, leaving many men to spend crucial years either struggling to meet child support obligations or facing the legal fallout from missed payments.

These financial pressures do more than strain a man's wallet; they can also prevent him from building a healthy relationship with his child. As the New Jersey State Senate recently noted, "Efforts to collect child support on behalf of children who have been removed from their parent's custody are often counterproductive... the added financial burden and possible legal consequences for the parents can often prove to be a barrier for reunification, even when it is the desired outcome and in the child's best interest." In other words, the very system meant to support the child can inadvertently make it harder for fathers to stay involved in their children's lives.

Compounding the issue, despite years since the Family and Medical Leave Act (FMLA) passage, companies are still more likely to offer maternity leave than paternity leave. This imbalance not only reflects the cultural bias toward mothers as primary caregivers but also limits fathers' ability to bond with their children from the start, deepening the challenges men face in fulfilling their parental roles.

The weight of child support and custody disputes often alters a man's freedom, shifts his goals, and complicates any future relationships he may hope to build. Many men start with dreams of financial independence, career goals, and even aspirations to provide for a family one day. But unplanned fatherhood brings an entirely new reality. When a man is ordered to make child support payments, his finances can quickly become shackled to monthly obligations that disrupt his ability to save, invest, or even change jobs freely. For some, this financial strain feels like a penalty on his freedom, his future tied to payments rather than to his own ambitions. The job he once took for growth opportunities or career advancement now has to be kept for its steady paycheck. The dreams of pursuing his passions and building a future on his terms take a backseat, replaced by the necessity of ensuring each payment goes through on time.

But the financial burden is only one piece. The emotional toll of custody disputes often reshapes a man's sense of self and how he approaches new relationships. Navigating a strained relationship with the mother of his child forces him to balance communication, cooperation, and respect, even if their history is marred by conflict. Every disagreement in court can feel like a test of his worthiness as a father and an exhausting cycle of proving himself capable of being present in his child's life. This ongoing emotional tug-of-war, coupled with the pain of missing out on his child's day-to-day life, can harden him or make him hesitant to open up to someone new. When he's already fighting to be a good dad from a distance, it can be hard to see where someone else would fit into a life so dictated by obligations he didn't anticipate.

Future relationships are often affected in more subtle yet lasting ways. A man involved in custody battles and child support arrangements will inevitably bring that experience into his next relationship, impacting how he sees partnership, commitment, and trust. The dynamic shifts; he's cautious about introducing his child to a new partner, and a part of him may hesitate to fully invest in a relationship knowing the stakes. He may question if his partner will stick with him through the hardships that accompany his role as a father. This reality can weigh heavily on a man's heart, leaving him questioning if his choice to have premarital sex was worth the ripple effect on his freedom, his future, and his relationships.

Extensive research highlights the pitfalls of cohabitation, showing that it often leads to significant financial loss and tends to reinforce a cycle of short-lived relationships that rarely move toward marriage. Studies suggest that cohabitation encourages "serial monogamy," where individuals engage in multiple cohabiting relationships over time without long-term commitment. Financial advisor Neasa MacErlean observes, "'Serial monogamy' is a way of life for many of today's twentysomethings, who often see cohabitation as a casual arrangement—a better option than living alone or staying with mom. Throughout their lives, many of today's young adults may live with four, five, or even six different partners."

Research organization Mintel also finds that cohabiting relationships are statistically more likely to dissolve than marriages, leaving many to return to single life before entering another cohabiting arrangement. Financial advisors highlight that financial protections are primarily designed for those legally married, not for cohabiting couples who share property, bank accounts, and large purchases without legal safeguards. This lack of protection can leave individuals financially vulnerable after a breakup, with assets and responsibilities divided inconsistently. Financial advisor Donna Bradshaw puts it plainly: "If you are in a long-term relationship—particularly if you have children—you are far better off being married."

Cohabitation without marriage may feel like an easy and flexible arrangement, but it often leads to significant property disputes, especially when joint purchases and shared assets come into play. When a couple shares a home, a car, or even furniture, these possessions can become sources of tension if the relationship ends. Unlike married couples, who are protected by legal frameworks to ensure fair distribution, cohabiting partners have no guaranteed legal pathway for dividing property equitably. This means that one person might walk away with a car they both paid for or lay claim to the apartment they shared, leaving the other partner in a challenging position—financially and emotionally.

Financial commitments can make the process even more challenging. Shared leases, co-signed debts, and loans are common in cohabiting relationships, but they come with serious strings attached if the relationship unravels. For instance, if one partner moves out, both parties may still be held financially responsible for the lease or debt, even if only one remains in the home. Debt collectors aren't interested in who broke up with whom; they're focused on payments. As a result, one partner might be on the hook for a loan taken out for joint purchases, like appliances or even vacations, while the other moves on without the financial baggage. These unresolved commitments can make it difficult to start fresh after the relationship ends.

Outside of marriage, the legal structure for dividing property and assets doesn't exist. This leaves former cohabitants vulnerable to uneven splits, emotional strain, and prolonged financial entanglements. For example, if a cohabiting couple shares a bank account and one partner decides to withdraw the funds, the other is left without a clear path to reclaim their portion. Similarly, when one partner has invested heavily in a shared property, they may walk away with nothing but receipts for a home they can no longer access. While marriage provides a layer of security through laws that address asset division, cohabitation leaves individuals to negotiate their own exit agreements— and these negotiations can be messy, drawn-out, and deeply personal. For many, this lack of structure leads to financial strain and lasting resentment, underscoring the risks of shared finances without the protection marriage provides.

As we near the end of this book, it's essential to take a moment for reflection—specifically on your current relationships and the choices you're making with your sexual lifestyle. At this point, it's vital to weigh the facts over fleeting emotions, convenience, or fear. Real, lasting change requires intentionality; there are

 Why men shouldn't have sex before marriage

countless people who love the idea of change but never put in the work to make it happen. And unfortunately, this might be true for some reading these very words. Many will finish this book and feel satisfied with just reading it, yet miss the mark of putting what they've learned into action. It's one of life's saddest ironies to know better yet fail to do better with what we've been given.

This book has equipped you with research, real-life testimonies, and scriptural support demonstrating that premarital sex, outside the commitment of marriage, is detrimental and burdensome. As I shared from the start, knowing the right thing brings a certain responsibility. Just as James 4:17 states, "So whoever knows the right thing to do and fails to do it, for him it is sin." This book isn't about imposing rules or mandates; rather, it's about presenting truths so that you now have a well-informed basis for your choices. You've been entrusted with the wisdom to make a decision that centers not just your satisfaction but also considers your future and those closely connected to your life.

So, let's evaluate with some questions: Is the relationship I'm currently in truly serving me and helping me become more like Jesus, moving me closer to the person I want to be? Am I in a relationship where only I hold the conviction to wait, while my partner doesn't? Are we both spiritually grounded and equally committed, sharing a foundation that can withstand life's challenges and go deeper than just physical satisfaction? If I've been with this person for a long time, what is keeping me from marriage? Am I afraid of missing out on someone better? Is there a fear of commitment, or do I feel that marriage is unnecessary since we're already acting as though we're married?

Ask yourself: Am I truly seeking a deeper relationship with Jesus, or am I content with a life that lacks spiritual commitment? Am I at risk of experiencing any of the long-term or short-term consequences we've discussed in this book? After reflecting on these questions, I challenge you to prayerfully consider your next steps. Some of you may have invested years into a relationship, and the thought of ending it is intimidating, as if all that time would be wasted. But the real question is, "Do I have more time to waste?" If you've put in this much time and nothing has progressed, what makes you think tomorrow will be any different?

Consider who you're surrounded by: Do you have anyone in your life who's taken a different path and is experiencing the fulfillment of it? Are there people in your life who hold you accountable or offer guidance based on their own lives and choices? Every man reading this must grapple with these questions. Being a responsible man means making decisions that aren't just about us but also impact others. Now, with the tools this book has provided, you're in a place to honestly assess your situation, consider your convictions, and make choices based on the truths presented.

 Why men shouldn't have sex before marriage

CONCLUSION

Taking the Next Step:
Moving Forward with Purpose

As I mentioned at the start of this book, I am an evangelist, and my purpose in writing it is twofold. First, I hope to inspire a generation of men to reclaim sexual purity, helping propel society toward a healthier way of life that opens hearts to the God who created us. Second, I desire to introduce you to Jesus Christ and invite you into a personal relationship with Him.

While salvation doesn't often occur in a single moment or at the "right" time, I am aware that seeds of faith may have already been planted in you long before you began reading these words. Some of you may already be familiar with the story of Jesus—His sacrifice on the cross, His resurrection, and the truth of Scripture. For others, this may be your first encounter with the gospel. Either way, it is a privilege to be part of this journey as God reveals Himself to you.

For those of you who have had seeds of faith sown and watered already, my prayer is that this book contributes to the growth of those seeds and helps you hear God's call more clearly. My hope is that, through these words, you will find the courage to surrender to Him and invite Him to lead your life.

These past eight chapters serve little purpose if you do not establish a personal relationship with Jesus, who empowers everything you've read here. While some may test my words and seek to prove them wrong, I trust that you'll recognize the love, commitment, and honesty in these pages. I desire to see you grow into the man God has created you to be, and if my obedience in writing this book has helped, I am deeply grateful.

Now, let me share the core message of the gospel, answering the question: "What must I do to be saved?" When a jailer asked this of Paul and Silas in Acts 16, they answered, "Believe in the Lord Jesus, and you will be saved—you and your household." I extend the same invitation to you:

Confess to God the ways you have gone your own way, living as if He didn't exist. Tell Him your regrets, your struggles, and your failures. Invite Him to forgive you and ask for His mercy. The God I serve is gracious and faithful to forgive those who repent. He desires to wrap you in His love and remind you that your debt is paid in full by His own sacrifice.

Believe that Jesus lived, died, and rose again for you. After confessing this belief, invite Him to fill your life with His Spirit, empowering you to live a life that pleases Him. Praise Him for receiving you as His child, knowing you're now part of the family of God.

If you've made this decision, congratulations. Here are some steps to support your journey:

1. Find Christian Community: Surround yourself with others who genuinely love Jesus—whether in a church, a campus ministry, or other groups. Even though no community is perfect, growing alongside others who share your faith will strengthen you. Commit to a body that loves Jesus and allows Him to work through that fellowship.

2. Commit to the Bible: Scripture is our guide and source of wisdom, and it reveals God's heart, His love, and His holiness. If the Bible felt distant or confusing before, now, with God's Spirit, it will come alive to you in new ways. Develop rhythms of studying the Bible individually and in groups, asking for understanding. God's Word will provide clarity, strength, and direction.

3. Prioritize Time with Jesus: Spend daily time in His presence. Whether in prayer, journaling, or worship, this practice humbles and transforms you. Find a consistent time, place, and routine, and make it a priority. Over time, you'll come to depend on this time with Him, feeling His love and closeness and recognizing that only He can truly satisfy your soul.

Glory be to God for those who come to know Him, restored and confident in both their spiritual and sexual lives. To God be the glory. Amen.

THE END

ABOUT THE AUTHOR

Cellus Hamilton is a hip-hop artist and minister based in Harlem, New York, where he lives with his wife Denya and their sons, Simeon and Marcellus. Raised in Atlanta, Cellus was surrounded by music and faith early on, inspired by his mother, who was also an artist. Today, he carries that torch by delivering bold messages of faith and purpose through his music, speaking, and ministry.

A well-traveled musician and Howard University alumnus, Cellus is passionate about influencing the culture and elevating conversations about faith, relationships, and purpose within the hip-hop community. He's also big on health and fitness, a lifelong fan of the Chicago Bulls and Kansas City Chiefs, and known as a "power nap" pro who somehow keeps a strict no-coffee rule. Beyond performing, Cellus spends time as a guest preacher across the U.S. and speaks in prisons, sports camps, and business summits.

When he's not writing or on stage, Cellus enjoys basketball, good food, and quality time with friends and family. He's devoted to mentoring young men, challenging them to pursue their potential and embrace God's vision for their lives—especially when it comes to the often-taboo subject of sexual purity. Through his music, speaking, and example, Cellus Hamilton continues to inspire people to seek true purpose, deeper connection, and faith-driven transformation.

ALSO AVAILABLE

Dive into the life and legacy of a hip-hop artist who started his rap career at age eight, growing up in the heart of the music industry. *If Jesus Was a Rapper* tells a unique story of perseverance, faith, and the power of hip-hop. This deeply personal memoir invites readers into the highs and lows of an artist who navigated both the challenges of adolescence and a relentless pursuit of his calling in the world of hip-hop.

In this compelling account, the author explores his journey of wrestling with trust in Jesus, detailing how every life experience—both good and challenging—served to deepen his faith and purpose. Through vivid storytelling, he parallels his life in hip-hop with the earthly ministry of Jesus, offering readers culturally relevant "parables" that bring the Bible to life in a new way for fans of hip-hop and urban culture.

Unique in its approach, *If Jesus Was a Rapper* challenges the music industry, Christian music culture, and the church's longstanding view on hip-hop's potential to reach and inspire. With a fresh perspective, this memoir sheds light on how rap can be a powerful tool for connecting people to Jesus, bridging cultural gaps, and engaging younger generations in kingdom principles.

Beyond its content, *If Jesus Was a Rapper* is a testament to hustle, having sold over 3,000 copies directly in the streets of NYC—on subways, buses, and street corners—and reaching readers across the nation during rap tours and through online bookstores. Independently published by Sow and Tell, this book is more than a memoir; it's a movement. Discover the story that's resonated with urban Christians and hip-hop fans alike, and experience what happens when faith and hip-hop collide.

 Why men shouldn't have sex before marriage